Badger Key Stage 3 ACE Science

Biology
Homework Tasks

**Dr Andrew Chandler-Grevatt &
Victoria Stutt**

CONTENTS

About the Authors

Dr Andrew Chandler-Grevatt

Andrew Grevatt is an experienced Advanced Skills Teacher and education author who currently trains teachers at the University of Sussex.

Victoria Stutt

Victoria is an experienced classroom teacher and educational author based in East Sussex, specialising in Chemistry.

INTRODUCTION

Introducing the new ACE Science Homework Tasks

So we have a new National Curriculum (2014), we have a programme of study, but no assessment guidance. To help teachers and students with this we have converted the previous Level Ladders into ACE Learning Ladders. Below, we remind you of the purpose of the homework activities, explain the ACE Learning Ladder and show how to use this book. We hope that you find these a useful addition to your teaching schemes.

Dr Andrew Chandler-Grevatt and Victoria Stutt

ACE Science Homework Tasks

It is often hard to set 'meaningful' homework tasks as it usually takes a lot of planning. These tasks have been developed to do just that: provide a range of extended homework projects from which students can get a much wider experience. We have found that many students relish the chance to 'do a project' and have a real feeling of pride with their work when they hand it in.

The key features of the ACE Science Homework Tasks:
- Extend learning outside the classroom.
- Encourage the use of science in 'real life' situations.
- Encourage independent learning.
- Encourage improvements in literacy, numeracy and ICT.
- Fit with the new 2014 KS3 Science Curriculum.
- Develop skills in working scientifically.
- Excellent preparation for Key Stage 4 assessment tasks.
- Allow parents to see not only how their children are being assessed but also the improvements in their work.

Cross-curricular opportunities

We feel that these projects could be easily adapted for such ventures and so have added some suggested links in the Teacher Notes. These tasks can be a starting point for this and we would be interested to know how people adapt and use these tasks for this part of the new Key Stage 3.

How and when?

We have written a general guide sheet for each type of task in addition to the specific advice in the Teacher Notes for each task.

These tasks can be used at any point throughout Biology teaching at Key Stage 3. We expect that teachers will use these tasks as a 'pick and mix'. For example, there are at least two tasks that could be used for a Relationships in an Ecosystem topic. You should choose tasks to best suit the class or even individuals within the class. Alternatively, there may be something in the news relevant to topics being covered, or a documentary that you would like your students to watch.

ACE Learning Ladders

We have introduced the ACE Learning Ladder, which can be used in a variety of ways to suit the needs or assessment system of your school.

A is for Advanced

The descriptors at this stage relate to the old levels 7 and 8 or an equivalent to grade A. They indicate that the student is working beyond the expectation of the National Curriculum for Key Stage 3.

C is for Confident

The descriptors at this stage relate to the old levels 5 and 6 or an equivalent to grade C. They indicate that the student is working at the expectation of the National Curriculum for Key Stage 3. From a 'mastery' perspective, students working at this stage have mastered this Key Stage 3 knowledge, understanding or skills within the programme of study.

E is for Establishing

The descriptors at this stage relate to the old levels 3 and 4 or an equivalent to grade E. They indicate that the student is currently working below the expectation of the National Curriculum for Key Stage 3. Students working at this stage will need support and intervention to become Confident.

How to use these tasks

Each task is a simple open-ended task that assesses knowledge and understanding of a significant concept from the new Science National Curriculum. The tasks should be photocopied with the task sheet and the ACE Learning Ladder back-to-back or side-to-side. Teachers and learners can use the ACE Learning Ladder to guide their response to the task.

Each task is available in three level ranges: Establishing, Confident and Advanced. This allows you to differentiate appropriately.

This book contains four types of task:
- Projects
- Making and Presenting
- Mini Investigations
- Critical Thinking.

General information on how to use each task is given on 'General Guide' sheets and specific information relating to each task is given in each task's 'Teacher Notes'.

Encouragement of use of ACE Learning Ladders

Some learners find it difficult to use the ACE Learning Ladder to guide their work. Strategies we have seen used include:
- encouraging the learner to tick or highlight the statements on the ACE Learning Ladder when they think they have satisfied them;
- using an exemplar and showing the students how to mark it using the ACE Learning Ladder.

ASSESSMENT OF THE ACE LEARNING TASKS

There are three approaches to assessing these tasks: teacher assessment, self-assessment and peer assessment.

Teacher assessment:

If you have not used these tasks before, we would recommend starting with the teacher assessment approach for assessing the learners' responses to the tasks. These are not like the standard tests or exams, where you have very clear guidance of what answers to accept and not accept. This approach is much more flexible and requires the use of professional judgement when assigning a level.

These tasks are not summative tests, so the level that is assigned to a learner's work is only a 'snapshot'. Learners often vary in their achievement from topic to topic. A good analogy to use with them is that of computer games. Computer games are often based on stages of success. Some people score more highly on some stages than others. The same will be experienced when doing the homework tasks. However, most learners show a general improvement trend when using these tasks.

The ACE Learning Ladders are written in learner-friendly language. These should be used when communicating achievement and progress with a learner. Additional guidance is given for teachers in the Teacher Notes – this should be used alongside the ACE Learning Ladder.

As with all new approaches, learners may need to do a few of these tasks before they get the full benefit from them. The tasks are very open and, to start with, some learners can feel overwhelmed by the freedom. They may need a lot of support and encouragement for the first few, but as their confidence grows the learners approach the tasks with more independence.

Do not get too bogged down in which grade to assign – make a judgement using the criteria, then assign the grade. We find that learners do pick up on anything they think has been badly judged! The resulting discussion is very useful to both parties.

Self-assessment and peer assessment

Encouraging learners to assess their own work or each others' can be very valuable. As with anything new, learners will need more guidance and support to start with before their confidence develops to do this successfully. We would highly recommend that time is taken to help learners develop these skills with the support of these tasks.

Self-assessment can be done by guiding learners through the ACE Learning Ladder and encouraging them to tick off the descriptors they feel they have satisfied. Then they can use the ACE Learning Ladder to help decide on suitable improvement targets. Peer assessment can be useful because learners can learn from each other as well as engage with what is required for each grade.

Generally, learners are reasonably accurate at assigning grades, but in self-assessment there is an issue in that they may not be aware of misconceptions that have been made. If you intend the learners to self-assess a piece of work in class, it is worth making sure that you challenge major misconceptions as you circulate.

GENERAL GUIDE: HOW TO USE THE PROJECTS

Purpose and focus

The Project tasks have been developed to:

- improve students' research skills and give them an opportunity to study a science topic that interests them in more depth
- extend learning outside the classroom
- give learners the opportunity to apply their knowledge and understanding in a given context
- encourage students to improve skills and scientific knowledge and understanding through an ACE Learning Ladder tailored to each task
- foster the research and literacy skills that are particularly important for projects carried out at KS4
- aid assessment for learning: teachers can assess the project at the end of the unit and give learners opportunities to make improvements through highlighted improvement strategies.

General approach

- Introduce the homework task at the start of the topic and set the final deadline.
- It is useful to set intermediate deadlines to check progress. Teachers who have used the tasks have found that checking progress once a week and contacting home if the student appears to have fallen behind on the task is effective.
- Collect in the projects at the agreed deadline.
- Mark the work using the Additional Guidance in the Teacher Notes as well as the ACE Learning Ladder. Some teachers like to tick off the statements that have been satisfied and highlight one or two statements as improvements.
- Any level given for the tasks should be a 'best fit' against the ACE Learning Ladder statements.
- On returning the tasks, give students an opportunity to make one improvement.

Expected time (Three homework sessions of between 30 and 60 minutes each)

Obviously this will depend on the ability of the students. Generally, these are intended to take three hours in total, made up of three one-hour sessions over three weeks. However, use your professional judgement to decide whether this should be reduced or extended.

Tailoring the tasks to your needs

The tasks can be easily adapted to suit the needs of your class, or to make it part of a cross-curricular project.

General Guide: How to use the Making and Presenting Tasks

Purpose and focus
The Making and Presenting tasks have been developed to:
- improve students' research skills and to give them an opportunity to develop their understanding through explanations of key ideas
- extend learning outside the classroom
- give learners the opportunity to apply their knowledge and understanding in a given context
- encourage students to improve skills and scientific knowledge and understanding through an ACE Learning Ladder tailored to each task
- aid assessment for learning: teachers can assess the project at the end of the unit and give learners opportunities to make improvements through highlighted improvement strategies.

General approach
- Introduce the homework task at the start of the topic and set the final deadline.
- It is useful to set intermediate deadlines to check progress. Teachers who have used the tasks have found that checking progress once a week and contacting home if the student appears to have fallen behind on the task is effective.
- Collect in the projects at the agreed deadline or set up a presentation session.
- Mark the work using the Additional Guidance in the Teacher Notes as well as the ACE Learning Ladder. Some teachers like to tick off the statements that have been satisfied and highlight one or two statements as improvements.
- Alternatively, encourage peer assessment of the presentations using the ACE Learning Ladders.
- Any level given for the tasks should be a 'best fit' against the ACE Learning Ladder statements.
- On returning the tasks, give students an opportunity to at least identify, if not make, one improvement.

Expected time (Three homework sessions of between 30 and 60 minutes each)
Obviously this will depend on the ability of the students. Generally, these are intended to take up to three hours. However, use your professional judgement to decide whether this should be reduced or extended.

Tailoring the tasks to your needs
The tasks can be easily adapted to suit the needs of your class, or to make it part of a cross-curricular project.

GENERAL GUIDE: HOW TO USE THE MINI INVESTIGATIONS

Purpose and focus
The Mini Investigations have been developed to:
- improve confidence in investigative skills, particularly in how to apply these to new problems/settings
- encourage students to carry out simple investigations at home using easily obtainable everyday items
- approach investigations independently, focusing on 'working scientifically'
- aid assessment for learning: teachers can assess the project at the end of the unit and give learners opportunities to make improvements through highlighted improvement strategies.

General approach
Note that schools may need to provide equipment for some students to use, although most investigations use equipment that can be found at home.

Health and Safety: It is essential that you discuss with your students any risks associated with an investigation. It is your responsibility to ensure that the tasks are adequately risk assessed. If you think your students are not responsible enough to work safely, then do not set the task.

- Introduce the homework task at the start of the topic and set the final deadline.
- It is useful to set intermediate deadlines to check progress. Teachers who have used the tasks have found that checking progress once a week and contacting home if the student appears to have fallen behind on the task is effective.
- Collect in the projects at the agreed deadline.
- Mark them using the Additional Guidance in the Teacher Notes as well as the ACE Learning Ladder. Some teachers like to tick off the statements that have been satisfied and highlight one or two statements as improvements.
- Any grade given for the tasks should be a 'best fit' against the ACE Learning Ladder statements.
- On returning the tasks, give students an opportunity to make one improvement.

Expected time (Three homework sessions of between 30 and 60 minutes each)
Obviously this will depend on the ability of the students. Generally, these are intended to take three hours in total, made up of three one-hour sessions over 3 weeks. However, use your professional judgement to decide whether this should be reduced or extended.

Tailoring the tasks to your needs
The tasks can be easily adapted to suit the needs of your class, or to make it part of a cross-curricular project.

GENERAL GUIDE: HOW TO USE THE CRITICAL THINKING TASKS

Purpose and focus
The Critical Thinking tasks have been designed to:
- develop skills for evaluating science-related news stories in the media
- help students begin to understand how scientific research is undertaken and how ideas change
- develop 'working scientifically' skills
- foster the research and literacy skills that are particularly important for projects carried out at KS4
- aid assessment for learning: teachers can assess the project at the end of the unit and give learners opportunities to make improvements through highlighted improvement strategies.

General approach
- Introduce the homework task at the start of the topic and set the final deadline.
- It is useful to set intermediate deadlines to check progress. Teachers who have used the tasks have found that checking progress once a week and contacting home if the student appears to have fallen behind on the task is effective.
- Collect in the projects at the agreed deadline.
- Mark them using the Additional Guidance in the Teacher Notes as well as the ACE Learning Ladder. Some teachers like to tick off the statements that have been satisfied and highlight one or two statements as improvements.
- Any grade given for the tasks should be a 'best fit' against the ACE Learning Ladder statements.
- On returning the tasks, give students an opportunity to make one improvement.

Expected time (Two homework sessions of between 30 and 60 minutes each)
Obviously this will depend on the ability of the students. Generally, these are intended to take two hours in total, made up of two one-hour sessions over two weeks. However, use your professional judgement to decide whether this should be reduced or extended.

Tailoring the tasks to your needs
The tasks can be easily adapted to suit the needs of your class, or to make it part of a cross-curricular project.

The Good Project Guide

Whenever you do research, use this research guide to get the best information.

Research tips

- Decide on **what** you are trying to find out.
- Decide on **keywords** that will be useful.
- Use the **internet, magazines** or **books** to find the information you need.
- Select the **relevant** information.
- Present the relevant information using your **own words**. Use tables or diagrams to present information and explain it.
- **List** all your sources of information in a **'Bibliography'** at the end of your work.

Literacy checklist

Make sure you have:
- Written with the **audience** in mind.
- Started each **sentence** with a **capital letter**.
- Written **correct sentences** (e.g. with full stops at the end, correct use of commas).
- Organised your sentences into **paragraphs**.
- Checked your **spelling** of simple words and science keywords.
- Used **apostrophes** to show contraction and possession.

Internet safety

Good internet research skills are valuable in the modern world. Be safe online! Use the websites your teacher suggests first, make sure your filters are set to 'safe', search responsibly, don't give out personal information and tell an adult or use the CEOP button if you find something that upsets you.

A good bibliography

A good bibliography allows the reader to find out exactly where you found the information.

Websites:
www.sciencestuff.com (date accessed) – do not just name your search engine!

Books:
A. Scientist (Year) Science for All. Publisher pp. 23-29.

Magazines:
Author Name (Year) Title of article, Title of Magazine, edition number, page numbers.

Read with caution

When reading information, think about the following things:

- When was it written?
- Who wrote it?
- Why did they write it?
- What evidence is used to support claims?
- Does the article contain facts or opinions?
- Is the source reliable?

Make sure you check information for bias (one-sided). If it is biased, try to find some information that takes the opposite view.

REPRODUCTION

- reproduction in humans (as an example of a mammal), including the structure and function of the male and female reproductive systems, menstrual cycle (without details of hormones), gametes, fertilisation, gestation and birth, to include the effect of maternal lifestyle on the fetus through the placenta.

INHERITANCE, CHROMOSOMES, DNA AND GENES

- heredity as the process by which genetic information is transmitted from one generation to the next
- differences between species.

CROSS–CURRICULAR OPPORTUNITIES INCLUDE:

- English – genres of writing and creative writing
- ICT – internet searching, word processing, use of PowerPoint
- mathematics – scale.

TIME

Three homework sessions of between 30 and 60 minutes each.

ASSESSMENT, FEEDBACK AND IMPROVEMENT

Assessing these tasks should not be arduous. Rather than assigning an absolute grade, you should focus on how each student can improve. To ensure that this task is formative, students should be given the opportunity to improve their work based on the teacher's targets or through peer and self-assessment.

GUIDANCE FOR CONFIDENT (C)

Students working with confidence will demonstrate an understanding of the relationship between the structure and function of organs and cells. The role of hormones should be included in the changes at puberty and birth (naming them and recognising that they influence the changes).

We find that reading through the project using these additional prompts helps to assess the task.

PROJECT 1: TASK SHEET (ESTABLISHING)
BABY BOOKLET

Young people have a lot of questions about the changes that occur as they grow up and need good scientific information to reassure them and help them make decisions.

Write an information booklet about the science of human reproduction and development.

Use websites, magazines and books to get information to answer each section below. Use the ACE Learning Ladder to help you do your best.

Use your own words throughout the project.

SECTION 1: GROWING UP
- Include information about the physical changes as boys and girls go through puberty.
- Describe some of the emotional changes that happen at puberty.
- Label a diagram of the reproductive system and describe the job of each part.

SECTION 2: MAKING A BABY
- Describe how humans reproduce.
- Suggest what couples should think about before deciding to have a baby.
- Draw diagrams and explain the terms 'fertilisation' and 'conception'.

SECTION 3: DEVELOPING AND BEING BORN
- Show and explain how a fetus develops in the uterus.
- Explain, simply, the role of the placenta.
- Describe how alcohol and smoking tobacco can affect the development of the fetus.
- Describe what happens at birth.

Use the Good Project Guide sheet for tips on internet safety, research and literacy.

PROJECT 1: TASK SHEET (CONFIDENT)
BABY BOOKLET

Young people have a lot of questions about the changes that occur as they grow up and need good scientific information to reassure them and help them make decisions.

Write an information booklet about the science of human reproduction and development.

Use websites, magazines and books to get information to answer each section below. Use the ACE Learning Ladder to help you do your best.

Use your own words throughout the project.

SECTION 1: GROWING UP
- Compare the physical changes that take place at puberty in both boys and girls.
- Describe some of the emotional changes that happen at puberty.
- Draw, label and explain diagrams of the male and female reproductive system.

SECTION 2: MAKING A BABY
- Describe how humans reproduce.
- Consider the issues involved with deciding to have a baby.
- Draw diagrams and explain the terms fertilisation and conception.

SECTION 3: DEVELOPING AND BEING BORN
- Show and explain how a fetus develops in the uterus.
- Explain, simply, the role of the placenta.
- Describe how alcohol and smoking tobacco can affect the development of the fetus.
- Describe what happens at birth.

Use the Good Project Guide sheet for tips on internet safety, research and literacy.

1 PROJECT 1: TASK SHEET (ADVANCED)
BABY BOOKLET

Young people have a lot of questions about the changes that occur as they grow up and need good scientific information to reassure them and help them make decisions.

Write an information booklet about the science of human reproduction and development.

Use websites, magazines and books to get information to answer each section below. Use the ACE Learning Ladder to help you do your best.

Use your own words throughout the project.

SECTION 1: GROWING UP
- Explain, in detail, the physical and emotional changes that take place at puberty in both boys and girls.
- Use labelled diagrams to explain the differences between the male and female reproductive systems.

SECTION 2: MAKING A BABY
- Describe how humans reproduce, explaining the terms fertilisation and conception.
- Consider the issues involved with deciding to have a baby.

SECTION 3: DEVELOPING AND BEING BORN
- Explain, in detail, the stages of pregnancy and birth, including how the unborn baby is supported by the mother's body.

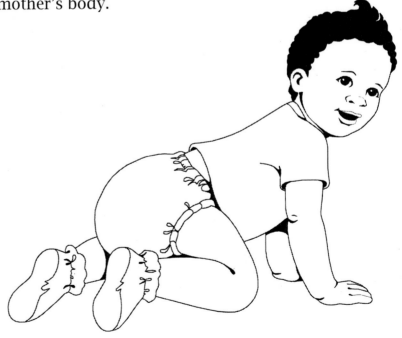

Use the Good Project Guide sheet for tips on internet safety, research and literacy.

BIOLOGY HOMEWORK TASKS: TASK SHEET (ADVANCED)

ACE LEARNING LADDER

Assessment Check	The types of things you can do:
Advanced	• Make an information booklet on human reproduction and development, drawing on detailed scientific knowledge and understanding. • Explain the stages of reproduction in the correct order, considering relative time scales. • Use detailed explanations and diagrams to show how the fetus develops. • Explain how unborn babies can be harmed while in the uterus, using data to support what you discuss, e.g. the risk to babies whose mothers smoke. • Use a range of appropriate scientific words, symbols and units accurately.
Confident	• Make an information booklet on human reproduction and development, drawing on scientific knowledge and understanding. • Explain how humans reproduce, using more than one step. • Explain how the fetus develops in the uterus. • Draw accurate diagrams to help explain the differences between the male and female reproductive system, in several sentences. • Explain the job of the placenta, the major stages of fetal development and birth using a range of keywords correctly. • Use a range of appropriate scientific words, symbols and units.
Establishing	• Make a simple information booklet about human reproduction and development, drawing on some scientific knowledge and understanding. • Give a simple description of how reproduction occurs. • Label the main parts of the female and male reproductive system. • Describe one or two changes boys and girls go through during puberty. • Name one or two substances that may harm an unborn baby. • Use some appropriate scientific words, symbols and units.

PROJECT 2: TEACHER NOTES
DOUBLE TROUBLE

REPRODUCTION
- reproduction in humans (as an example of a mammal), including the structure and function of the male and female reproductive systems, menstrual cycle (without details of hormones), gametes, fertilisation, gestation and birth, to include the effect of maternal lifestyle on the fetus through the placenta.

INHERITANCE, CHROMOSOMES, DNA AND GENES
- heredity as the process by which genetic information is transmitted from one generation to the next
- differences between species.

WORKING SCIENTIFICALLY
Analysis and evaluation

CROSS–CURRICULAR OPPORTUNITIES INCLUDE:
- English – informative writing
- ICT – internet searching, word processing.

TIME

Three homework sessions of between 30 and 60 minutes each.

ASSESSMENT, FEEDBACK AND IMPROVEMENT

Assessing these tasks should not be arduous. Rather than assigning an absolute grade, you should focus on how each student can improve. To ensure that this task is formative, students should be given the opportunity to improve their work based on the teacher's targets or through peer and self-assessment.

GUIDANCE FOR CONFIDENT (C)

Through completing this task, students should be able to explain, using diagrams to aid them, how identical and non-identical twins occur. Students working beyond Confident (C) should also be able to explain cloning and examine some of the ethical issues behind the procedure.

PROJECT 2: TASK SHEET (ESTABLISHING)
DOUBLE TROUBLE

Do you know any twins? You may know twins who are identical or perhaps twins who look, and even behave, nothing like one another. So why do twins occur?

Find out how identical twins and non-identical twins are formed.
Make a visual guide on this for other students which explains how twins are formed.
Include a few sentences to describe or explain each picture.

Use websites, magazines and books to get information to answer each section below. Use the ACE Learning Ladder to help you do your best.

Use your own words throughout the project.

SECTION 1: HOW ARE TWINS FORMED?
- Describe how twins are formed.
- Describe the difference between identical and non-identical twins.
- Use diagrams to show how both types of twins are made when egg cells and sperm cells meet.

SECTION 2: WHAT DOES IT MEAN TO HAVE TWINS?
- List the things that new parents need to think about and do if they have twins.
- List the reasons for people to having twins (e.g. does it run in families?)

SECTION 3: WHAT ARE CONJOINED TWINS?
- Describe what conjoined twins are.
- Explain, using a simple diagram, how conjoined twins form.
- Explain, simply, the issues that doctors and parents face when conjoined twins are born.

Use the Good Project Guide sheet for tips on internet safety, research and literacy.

DOUBLE TROUBLE

Do you know any twins? You may know twins who are identical or perhaps twins who look, and even behave, nothing like one another. So why do twins occur?

Find out how identical twins and non-identical twins are formed. Prepare a visual guide on this for other students, showing what happens at fertilisation to make twins.

Use websites, magazines and books to get information to answer each section below. Use the ACE Learning Ladder to help you do your best.

Use your own words throughout the project.

SECTION 1: HOW ARE TWINS FORMED?
- Explain how twins are formed.
- Compare identical and non-identical twins.
- Use diagrams to show how both types of twins are made when egg cells and sperm cells meet.

SECTION 2: WHAT DOES IT MEAN TO HAVE TWINS?
- Discuss the things that new parents need to think about and do if they have twins.
- Find out if there are any reasons for people having twins (e.g. does it run in families?)

SECTION 3: WHAT ARE CONJOINED TWINS?
- Describe what conjoined twins are.
- Explain, using a diagram, how conjoined twins form.
- Explain the issues that doctors and parents face when conjoined twins are born.

Use the Good Project Guide sheet for tips on internet safety, research and literacy.

BIOLOGY HOMEWORK TASKS: TASK SHEET (CONFIDENT)

PROJECT 2: TASK SHEET (ADVANCED)
DOUBLE TROUBLE

Do you know any twins? You may know twins who are identical or perhaps twins who look, and even behave, nothing like one another. So why do twins occur?

Find out how identical twins and non-identical twins are formed. Prepare a visual guide on this for other students, showing what happens at fertilisation to make twins.

Use websites, magazines and books to get information to answer each section below. Use the ACE Learning Ladder to help you do your best.

Use your own words throughout the project.

Set your visual guide out in the following sections:

Section 1: How are identical and non-identical twins formed?

Section 2: What does it mean to have twins and why do people have them?

Section 3: What are conjoined twins?

You might include:
• Examples of famous conjoined twins.

Use the Good Project Guide sheet for tips on internet safety, research and literacy.

ACE LEARNING LADDER

Assessment Check	The types of things you can do:
Advanced	• Produce a detailed visual guide, drawing on detailed scientific knowledge and understanding. • Explain, in detail, how identical and non-identical twins are formed, in terms of the cells involved, what happens at fertilisation and the genetic make-up of twins. • Explain complications that may occur during pregnancy, birth and infanthood as a result of having twins. • Explain the likelihood of having twins, using evidence to support your answers. • Identify and discuss issues surrounding separation of conjoined twins, justifying all points made with evidence. • Use a range of appropriate scientific words, symbols and units accurately.
Confident	• Produce a visual guide, drawing on scientific knowledge and understanding. • Explain how identical and non-identical twins are formed, in terms of the cells involved and what happens at fertilisation. • Explain how pregnancy and birth involving twins may be different to that of a single baby. • Explain why some people have twins and the considerations for families of twins. • Identify and discuss issues surrounding separation of conjoined twins. • Use a range of appropriate scientific words, symbols and units.
Establishing	• Make a simple visual guide, drawing on some scientific knowledge and understanding. • Describe in simple terms how identical and non-identical twins are made during fertilisation. • State one or two ways pregnancy and birth may be different for twins. • State two considerations parents expecting twins would need to make. • Describe, simply, how conjoined twins are formed and why separation may be wanted or needed. • Use some appropriate scientific words, symbols and units.

PROJECT 3: TEACHER NOTES
BRITISH MAMMAL PROJECT

NATIONAL CURRICULUM LINKS

RELATIONSHIPS IN AN ECOSYSTEM
- the interdependence of organisms in an ecosystem, including food webs and insect pollinated crops
- how organisms affect, and are affected by, their environment, including the accumulation of toxic materials.

WORKING SCIENTIFICALLY
Analysis and evaluation

CROSS–CURRICULAR OPPORTUNITIES INCLUDE:
- ICT – internet searching, word processing
- geography – environment and UK habitats.

TIME

Three homework sessions of between 30 and 60 minutes each.

ASSESSMENT, FEEDBACK AND IMPROVEMENT

Assessing these tasks should not be arduous. Rather than assigning an absolute grade, you should focus on how each student can improve. To ensure that this task is formative, students should be given the opportunity to improve their work based on the teacher's targets or through peer and self-assessment.

GUIDANCE FOR CONFIDENT (C)

Students working with confidence will have devised their simple food web of at least five organisms and recognised and discussed that the adaptations are related to the mammal's survival. For students working at Advanced (A) stages, the food web is likely to be complex and used to explain the threats to the population. Adaptations will include internal, external and behavioural features, with detailed explanations linking to survival.

We find that reading through the project using these additional prompts helps to assess the task.

PROJECT 3: TASK SHEET (ESTABLISHING)
BRITISH MAMMAL PROJECT

Write a report about the life of a British mammal of your choice.

The aim of this project is for you to be able to select information, use scientific knowledge and understanding to describe the mammal's habitat and adaptations, and to explain its feeding relationships.

Use websites, magazines and books to get information to answer each section below. Use the ACE Learning Ladder to help you do your best.

Use your own words throughout the project.

SECTION 1: HABITAT AND LIFE CYCLE
- Name the mammal you are studying. (Has it got a scientific name?)
- Describe the mammal's habitat; include a picture.
- Describe how the habitat changes through the year.
- Describe the mammal's life cycle.
- Can you find out how many of this mammal there are in the UK? Where do they mainly live?

SECTION 2: ADAPTATIONS
- Describe how the mammal is adapted to survive in its habitat.
- Describe how it feeds, stays warm, catches food and escapes predators.
- Include a picture of the mammal. State reasons for its adaptations.

SECTION 3: FOOD CHAINS AND WEBS
- Describe what your mammal eats. Is it a herbivore or carnivore?
- Is your mammal prey to any predators? What are they?
- Draw a food chain or web that includes the mammal.
- Describe any threats there are to the population of the mammal.

Use the Good Project Guide sheet for tips on internet safety, research and literacy.

BIOLOGY HOMEWORK TASKS: TASK SHEET (ESTABLISHING)

1 PROJECT 3: TASK SHEET (CONFIDENT)
BRITISH MAMMAL PROJECT

Write a report about the life of a British mammal of your choice.

The aim of this project is for you to be able to select information, use scientific knowledge and understanding to describe the mammal's habitat and adaptations, and to explain its feeding relationships.

Use websites, magazines and books to get information to answer each section below. Use the ACE Learning Ladder to help you do your best.

Use your own words throughout the project.

SECTION 1: HABITAT AND LIFE CYCLE
- Name the mammal you are studying. (Has it got a scientific name?)
- Describe the mammal's habitat; include a picture.
- Describe the seasonal changes which occur in the habitat.
- Describe the mammal's life cycle.
- What is the distribution of the mammal? Include a map if you can.

SECTION 2: ADAPTATIONS
- Explain how the mammal is adapted to survive in its habitat. Explain how it feeds, stays warm, catches prey, escapes predators, etc.
- Include a picture of the mammal. Give reasons for the adaptations.

SECTION 3: FOOD CHAINS AND WEBS
- Describe what your mammal eats. Is it a herbivore or carnivore?
- Is your mammal prey to any predators? What are they?
- Draw an accurate food chain or web that includes the mammal.
- Describe any threats there are to the population of the mammal.

Use the Good Project Guide sheet for tips on internet safety, research and literacy.

BIOLOGY HOMEWORK TASKS: TASK SHEET (CONFIDENT)

PROJECT 3: TASK SHEET (ADVANCED)
BRITISH MAMMAL PROJECT

Write a report about the life of a British mammal of your choice.

The aim of this project is for you to be able to select information, use scientific knowledge and understanding to describe the mammal's habitat and adaptations, and to explain its feeding relationships.

Use websites, magazines and books to get information to answer each section below. Use the ACE Learning Ladder to help you do your best.

Use your own words throughout the project.

SECTION 1: HABITAT AND LIFE CYCLE
- Name the mammal, using both its common and scientific names.
- Describe the mammal's habitat and how this changes over time (daily, seasonally and historically).
- Explain the life cycle of the mammal and its distribution and population within the UK.

SECTION 2: ADAPTATIONS
- Include suitable pictures and diagrams of the mammal.
- Explain in detail how the mammal is adapted to survive in its habitat and why these adaptations are important.

SECTION 3: FOOD CHAINS AND WEBS
- Design a food chain and food web to show what your mammal eats, and which organisms eat your mammal.
- Describe and explain the mammal's position in the food web, using scientific vocabulary.
- Describe and explain any past, present and future threats there are to the population of the mammal. Predict and evaluate the future of the mammal.

Use the Good Project Guide sheet for tips on internet safety, research and literacy.

BIOLOGY HOMEWORK TASKS: TASK SHEET (ADVANCED)

BRITISH MAMMAL PROJECT

ACE Learning Ladder

Assessment Check	The types of things you can do:
Advanced	• Write a detailed report on a British mammal of your choice, drawing on detailed scientific knowledge and understanding. • Explain how the mammal is adapted to its habitat. • Explain how and why the mammal's population changes over time and how the population is distributed across the UK. • Explain how the mammal's population has changed and predict how it may change in the near future, giving detailed reasons. • Design a food web that contains the mammal and correctly identifies each trophic level and classifies each organism. • Use a range of scientific words, symbols and units accurately.
Confident	• Write a report on a British mammal of your choice, drawing on scientific knowledge and understanding. • Explain what the habitat of your mammal is like and how it changes through the seasons. • Explain how your British mammal is adapted to survive in its habit. • Draw and explain a food web that includes your mammal. • Use a range of appropriate scientific words, symbols and units.
Establishing	• Write a simple report on a mammal of your choice, drawing on some scientific knowledge and understanding. • Give a simple description of the mammal's habitat, including a picture. • State one or two ways your mammal is adapted to survive. • Give one food chain involving your mammal and possibly place this within a simple food web. • Use some appropriate scientific words, symbols and units.

1

PROJECT 4: TEACHER NOTES
ENDANGERED ANIMALS

RELATIONSHIPS IN AN ECOSYSTEM
- the interdependence of organisms in an ecosystem, including food webs and insect pollinated crops
- how organisms affect, and are affected by, their environment, including the accumulation of toxic materials.

WORKING SCIENTIFICALLY
Analysis and evaluation

CROSS–CURRICULAR OPPORTUNITIES INCLUDE:
- geography – knowledge of animals' wider habitats
- citizenship – preserving the natural environment.

TIME

Three homework sessions of between 30 and 60 minutes each.

ADDITIONAL GUIDANCE

This task offers great scope for students to research any endangered animal they are interested in. They will need to use their knowledge of feeding relationships and habitats when describing the animal's place in any ecosystem. They will also need to consider threats to the animal from both natural and human causes.

ASSESSMENT, FEEDBACK AND IMPROVEMENT

Assessing these tasks should not be arduous. Rather than assigning an absolute grade, you should focus on how each student can improve. To ensure that this task is formative, students should be given the opportunity to improve their work based on the teacher's targets or through peer and self-assessment.

GUIDANCE FOR CONFIDENT (C)

Students working with confidence should be able to carry out an internet search, describe the animal, explain its main adaptations and identify its place within any ecosystem, using a food web.

We find that reading through the project using these additional prompts helps to assess the task.

Many species are under threat and could soon become extinct. You are going to research an endangered animal of your choice and prepare a PowerPoint for a conservation charity.

You should find out about the animal's habitat, feeding relationships and adaptations. Your presentation should include any threats to the animal's survival, along with steps being taken to preserve its numbers, or measures you believe should be taken to help it.

Use websites, magazines and books to get information to answer each section below. Use the ACE Learning Ladder to help you do your best.

Use your own words throughout the project.

SECTION 1: HABITAT
- Name the animal you are studying. (Has it got a scientific name?)
- Describe the animal's habitat; include a picture.
- Where in the world does the animal live? Can you find out how many there are?

SECTION 2: ADAPTATIONS AND FEEDING
- Include a picture of the animal. Identify its adaptations.
- Describe what your animal eats. Is it a herbivore or carnivore?
- Is your animal prey to any predators? What are they?
- Draw a food chain or web which includes the animal.
- Draw a pyramid of numbers or biomass (estimated!).

SECTION 3: THREATS AND CONSERVATION
- What is the current population of the animal? How has it changed?
- Describe the threats that there are to the animal.
- Describe any conservation work that is being done to save the animal from extinction.

Use the Good Project Guide sheet for tips on internet safety, research and literacy.

1 PROJECT 4: TASK SHEET (CONFIDENT)
ENDANGERED ANIMALS

Many species are under threat and could soon become extinct. You are going to research an endangered animal of your choice and prepare a PowerPoint for a conservation charity.

You should find out about the animal's habitat, feeding relationships and adaptations. Your presentation should include any threats to the animal's survival, along with steps being taken to preserve its numbers, or measures you believe should be taken to help it.

Use websites, magazines and books to get information to answer each section below. Use the ACE Learning Ladder to help you do your best.

Use your own words throughout the project.

SECTION 1: HABITAT
- Name the animal you are studying. (Has it got a scientific name?)
- Describe the animal's habitat; include a picture.
- What is the distribution of the animal? Include a map if you can.

SECTION 2: ADAPTATIONS AND FEEDING
- Include a picture of the animal. Identify its adaptations.
- Describe what your animal eats. Is it a herbivore or carnivore?
- Is your animal prey to any predators? What are they?
- Draw a food chain or web which includes the animal.
- Draw a pyramid of numbers or biomass (estimated!).

SECTION 3: THREATS AND CONSERVATION
- What is the population of the animal? How has it changed?
- Describe the threats that there are to the animal.
- Describe any conservation work that is being done to save the animal from extinction.

Use the Good Project Guide sheet for tips on internet safety, research and literacy.

BIOLOGY HOMEWORK TASKS: TASK SHEET (CONFIDENT)

1

PROJECT 4: TASK SHEET (ADVANCED)
ENDANGERED ANIMALS

Many species are under threat and could soon become extinct. You are going to research an endangered animal of your choice and prepare a PowerPoint for a conservation charity.

You should find out about the animal's habitat, feeding relationships and adaptations. Your presentation should include any threats to the animal's survival, along with steps being taken to preserve its numbers, or measures you believe should be taken to help it. Include information on the current population of the animal and how this population has changed over time.

Decide on the best way to set out your PowerPoint. Make the information you give easy to read and remember.

Use websites, magazines and books to get information to answer each section below. Use the ACE Learning Ladder to help you do your best.

Use your own words throughout the project.

SECTION 1: HABITAT
- Name the animal you are studying. (Has it got a scientific name?)
- Describe the animal's habitat; include a picture.
- What is the distribution of the animal? Include a map if you can.

SECTION 2: ADAPTATIONS AND FEEDING
- Include a picture of the animal. Identify its adaptations.
- Describe what your animal eats. Is it a herbivore or carnivore?
- Is your animal prey to any predators? What are they?
- Draw a food chain or web which includes the animal.
- Draw a pyramid of numbers or biomass (estimated!).

SECTION 3: THREATS AND CONSERVATION
- What is the population of the animal? How has it changed?
- Describe the threats that there are to the animal.
- Describe any conservation work that is being done to save the animal from extinction.

Use the Good Project Guide sheet for tips on internet safety, research and literacy.

BIOLOGY HOMEWORK TASKS: TASK SHEET (ADVANCED)

ACE LEARNING LADDER

Assessment Check	The types of things you can do:
Advanced	• Make a detailed PowerPoint, drawing on detailed scientific knowledge and understanding. • Write a detailed presentation of at least eight slides, including relevant diagrams. • Explain how your animal is adapted to several aspects of its habitat. • Explain your animal's place in the ecosystem, using food chains, food webs and accurate pyramids of numbers. • Explain the steps conservationists are taking to conserve the animal, using evidence to show the impact (positive or negative) these are having. • Use a range of scientific words, symbols and units accurately.
Confident	• Make a PowerPoint, drawing on scientific knowledge and understanding. • Write a 6-8 slide presentation, including relevant diagrams. • Explain how your animal is adapted to its habitat. • Explain your animal's place in the ecosystem, using food chains and food webs. • Explain the steps conservationists are taking to conserve the animal. • Use a range of appropriate scientific words, symbols and units.
Establishing	• Make a simple PowerPoint, drawing on some scientific knowledge and understanding. • Write a 3-4 slide presentation, including diagrams. • State some of your animal's adaptations. • Draw a simple food chain or web involving your animal's. • State some steps conservationists are using to conserve your animal. • Use some appropriate scientific words, symbols and units.

PROJECT 5: TEACHER NOTES
PROFITABLE PLANTS

NATIONAL CURRICULUM LINKS

RELATIONSHIPS IN AN ECOSYSTEM
- the interdependence of organisms in an ecosystem, including food webs and insect pollinated crops
- the importance of plant reproduction through insect pollination in human food security.

GAS EXCHANGE SYSTEMS
- the role of leaf stomata in gas exchange in plants.

REPRODUCTION
- reproduction in plants, including flower structure, wind and insect pollination, fertilisation, seed and fruit formation and dispersal, including quantitative investigation of some dispersal mechanisms.

NUTRITION AND DIGESTION
- plants making carbohydrates in their leaves by photosynthesis and gaining mineral nutrients and water from the soil via their roots.

WORKING SCIENTIFICALLY
Analysis and evaluation

CROSS-CURRICULAR OPPORTUNITIES INCLUDE:
- food technology – knowledge of food substances
- geography – maps and biomes.

TIME

Three homework sessions of between 30 and 60 minutes each.

ADDITIONAL GUIDANCE

This task could be used as an introduction to a plant topic, or within any topic dealing with food groups or plant structure. Students will first need to find out the parts of plants which can be eaten, e.g. tuber, seeds, etc. They will then need to categorise several common examples of plants of their choosing. You may like to provide a keyword list showing the main parts of plants for Establishing (E) students to use as a basis for their research. Students should also be familiar with the role insects play in pollination and how this in turn affects food security for humans.

ASSESSMENT, FEEDBACK AND IMPROVEMENT

Assessing these tasks should not be arduous. Rather than assigning an absolute grade, you should focus on how each student can improve. To ensure that this task is formative, students should be given the opportunity to improve their work based on the teacher's targets or through peer and self-assessment.

GUIDANCE FOR CONFIDENT (C)

Students working with confidence will be able to carry out targeted research into the parts of a plant and identify some common examples.

We find that reading through the project using these additional prompts helps to assess the task.

PROFITABLE PLANTS

We all know that we should eat at least five portions of fruit and vegetables each day, but do you know very much about the fruits and vegetables you eat? Where do these plants come from? Who discovered them? How have they come to be an important part of our diet?

Examples: potatoes, wheat, coffee, tea, sugar cane, cocoa, rice

Prepare a booklet about the plant and its discovery and uses.

Use websites, magazines and books to get information to answer each section below. Use the ACE Learning Ladder to help you do your best.

Use your own words throughout the project.

SECTION 1: INTRODUCING THE PLANT
- Use the internet to find out about the plant you have chosen.
- Draw a diagram of a plant, identifying where each part is.
- Give some information about what each plant part does.

SECTION 2: HOW IS IT GROWN AND HARVESTED?
- Find out where the plant is grown.
- Describe and explain how the plant is grown.
- Describe and explain how the plant is harvested and which parts are used.

SECTION 3: HISTORY OF THE DISCOVERY AND THE USE OF THE PLANT
- Describe when the plant was first used for food.
- Describe how the plant was discovered, when and by whom.
- Explain how the plant's use and harvest have developed with changing technology.

SECTION 4: FOOD SECURITY
- Describe how insects may help more of the plant to grow.
- Describe how we would be affected if fewer insects were available to help more plants grow.
- Describe some other problems that could affect how much of the plant is able to be used as food.

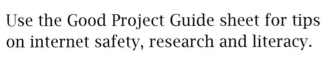

Use the Good Project Guide sheet for tips on internet safety, research and literacy.

PROJECT 5: TASK SHEET (CONFIDENT)
PROFITABLE PLANTS

We all know that we should eat at least five portions of fruit and vegetables each day, but do you know very much about the fruits and vegetables you eat? Where do these plants come from? Who discovered them? How have they come to be an important part of our diet?

Examples: potatoes, wheat, coffee, tea, sugar cane, cocoa, rice

Prepare a booklet about the plant and its discovery and uses.

Use websites, magazines and books to get information to answer each section below. Use the ACE Learning Ladder to help you do your best.

Use your own words throughout the project.

SECTION 1: INTRODUCING THE PLANT
- Use the internet to find out about the plant you have chosen.
- Draw a diagram of a plant, identifying where each part is.
- Give some information about what each plant part does.

SECTION 2: HOW IS IT GROWN AND HARVESTED?
- Find out where the plant is grown.
- Describe and explain how the plant is grown.
- Describe and explain how the plant is harvested and which parts are used.

SECTION 3: HISTORY OF THE DISCOVERY AND THE USE OF THE PLANT
- Describe when the plant was first used for food.
- Describe how the plant was discovered, when and by whom.
- Explain how the plant's use and harvest have developed with changing technology.

SECTION 4: FOOD SECURITY
- Describe what is meant by the term 'food security'.
- Describe how insects affect the food security of the plant you have chosen.
- Describe some other issues that may have an impact on the food security of your plant.

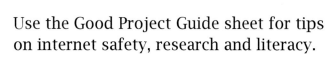

Use the Good Project Guide sheet for tips on internet safety, research and literacy.

BIOLOGY HOMEWORK TASKS: TASK SHEET (CONFIDENT)

PROJECT 5: TASK SHEET (ADVANCED)
PROFITABLE PLANTS

We all know that we should eat at least five portions of fruit and vegetables each day, but do you know very much about the fruits and vegetables you eat? Where do these plants come from? Who discovered them? How have they come to be an important part of our diet?

Examples: potatoes, wheat, coffee, tea, sugar cane, cocoa, rice

Prepare a booklet about the plant, its discovery and uses and its importance for food security.

Use websites, magazines and books to get information to answer each section below. Use the ACE Learning Ladder to help you do your best.

Use your own words throughout the project.

Divide your booklet into the following sections:

SECTION 1: INTRODUCING THE PLANT
- Include detailed diagrams and descriptions of your chosen plant, including its structure and uses.

SECTION 2: HOW IS IT GROWN AND HARVESTED?
- Include detailed descriptions of all the stages of growing and harvesting.

SECTION 3: HISTORY OF THE DISCOVERY AND THE USE OF THE PLANT
- Give a detailed history of how the plant came to be used for its current purposes.

SECTION 4: THE IMPORTANCE OF THE PLANT TO FOOD SECURITY
- Explain in detail how the plant you have chosen impacts on food security.

Use the Good Project Guide sheet for tips on internet safety, research and literacy.

PROJECT 5: ACE LEARNING LADDER
PROFITABLE PLANTS

ACE LEARNING LADDER

Assessment Check	The types of things you can do:
Advanced	• Write a detailed booklet, drawing on detailed scientific knowledge and understanding. • Draw a detailed labelled diagram of the plant and another to show the different cells that would be observed if seen under a microscope. • Explain the conditions needed for the plant to grow and link this to the main places the plant is grown globally. • Explain how the plant was first discovered and grown and how this has changed over time, explaining how this links with scientific advances in areas such as agriculture or technology. • Explain in detail how insects play a part in food security and how important your plant is as a food source worldwide. • Use a range of scientific words, symbols and units accurately.
Confident	• Write a booklet, drawing on scientific knowledge and understanding. • Draw a detailed labelled diagram of the plant, including some of the cells present. • Explain the conditions needed for the plant to grow. • Explain how the plant was first discovered and grown and how this has changed over time. • Explain the significance of your plant, and of insects, to food security. • Use a range of appropriate scientific words, symbols and units.
Establishing	• Write a simple booklet, drawing on some scientific knowledge and understanding. • Draw a labelled diagram of the plant. • State the things the plant would need to be able to grow. • State where and when the plant was discovered and how it was first used. • Describe what food security is and the role insects have in it. • Use some appropriate scientific words, symbols and units.

NATIONAL CURRICULUM LINKS

The topic covered will depend on the practical examples students focus on.

WORKING SCIENTIFICALLY
Scientific attitudes
Experimental skills and investigations
Analysis and evaluation

TIME

Three homework sessions of between 30 and 60 minutes each.

ADDITIONAL GUIDANCE

Students will need to have experience of planning and carrying out practical investigations. This task will help students to consider the essential principles of investigations that allow valid and reliable results to be collected. You may wish to choose a suitable investigation for Establishing students to base their work on, and provide prompts about how the investigation would need to be set up. Students should have met the keywords in the task – objectivity, validity, accuracy, precision and uncertainty.

ASSESSMENT, FEEDBACK AND IMPROVEMENT

Assessing these tasks should not be arduous. Rather than assigning an absolute grade, you should focus on how each student can improve. To ensure that this task is formative, students should be given the opportunity to improve their work based on the teacher's targets or through peer and self-assessment.

GUIDANCE FOR CONFIDENT (C)

Students working with confidence can present two perspectives and justify their own viewpoint.

We find that reading through the project using these additional prompts helps to assess the task.

Every day, scientists carry out investigations. It is important that they work scientifically, so that any results they obtain can be trusted. You may have carried out your own investigation and thought about how to make it a 'fair test'. But what does that actually mean?

Produce a poster that could be displayed in your school laboratory to help other students make sure they are always working scientifically.

Your teacher will show you a practical investigation that you should use as an example when discussing how to work scientifically.

Think about the following points when you design your poster:
- Why is it important that scientists always work scientifically?
- What do the following words mean – objectivity, precision, accuracy, repeatability and reproducibility?
- How would a scientist make sure their investigation was objective?
- What does it mean if results are precise? How could you make sure results in your experiment are precise?
- What does it mean if results are accurate? How could you make sure results in your experiment are accurate?
- Why is it important for investigations to be repeatable or reproducible? How would you ensure this in your example investigation?

Use the ACE Learning Ladder to help you do your best.

Use your own words throughout the project.

Use the Good Project Guide sheet for tips on internet safety, research and literacy.

BIOLOGY HOMEWORK TASKS: TASK SHEET (ESTABLISHING)

PROJECT 6: TASK SHEET (CONFIDENT)
STAYING SCIENTIFIC

Every day, scientists carry out investigations. It is important that they work scientifically, so that any results they obtain can be trusted. You may have carried out your own investigation and thought about how to make it a 'fair test'. But what does that actually mean?

Produce a poster that could be displayed in your school laboratory to help other students make sure they are always working scientifically.

Think of an investigation you have carried out before that would be a good way to illustrate how to work scientifically.

Think about the following points when you design your poster:
• Why is it important that scientists always work scientifically?
• What do the following words mean – objectivity, precision, accuracy, repeatability and reproducibility?
• How would a scientist make sure their investigation was objective and would give valid results?
• What does it mean if results are precise? How could you make sure results in your experiment are precise?
• What does it mean if results are accurate? How could you make sure results in your experiment are accurate?
• Why is it important for investigations to be repeatable or reproducible? How would you ensure this in your example investigation?

Use the ACE Learning Ladder to help you do your best.

Use your own words throughout the project.

Use the Good Project Guide sheet for tips on internet safety, research and literacy.

BIOLOGY HOMEWORK TASKS: TASK SHEET (CONFIDENT)

PROJECT 6: TASK SHEET (ADVANCED)
STAYING SCIENTIFIC

Every day, scientists carry out investigations. It is important that they work scientifically, so that any results they obtain can be trusted. You may have carried out your own investigation and thought about how to make it a 'fair test'. But what does that actually mean?

Produce a poster that could be displayed in your school laboratory to help other students make sure they are always working scientifically.

Think of an investigation you have carried out before that would be a good way to illustrate how to work scientifically. It is up to you how to set your poster out, but you must explain what the following words mean, and explain how you would ensure they were in place in your example investigation:

- Objectivity
- Precision
- Accuracy
- Repeatability
- Reproducibility

Use the ACE Learning Ladder to help you do your best.

Use your own words throughout the project.

Use the Good Project Guide sheet for tips on internet safety, research and literacy.

BIOLOGY HOMEWORK TASKS: TASK SHEET (ADVANCED)

STAYING SCIENTIFIC

ACE LEARNING LADDER

Assessment Check	The types of things you can do:
Advanced	• Produce a detailed poster, drawing on detailed scientific knowledge and understanding. • Explain the words objectivity, precision, accuracy, repeatability and reproducibility in terms of scientific investigations, using examples to explain their meaning. • Choose a suitable investigation and sample set of results to highlight each of these points. • Explain how to ensure these are present in all investigations. • Identify an example of an investigation where objectivity, precision, reliability and reproducibility were not present and explain the consequences of this. • Use a range of scientific words, symbols and units accurately.
Confident	• Produce a poster, drawing on scientific knowledge and understanding. • Explain the words objectivity, precision, accuracy, repeatability and reproducibility in terms of scientific investigations. • Choose a suitable investigation to highlight each of these points. • Explain how to ensure these are present in your example investigation. • Explain the consequences of investigations not being carried out scientifically. • Use a range of appropriate scientific words, symbols and units.
Establishing	• Produce a simple poster, drawing on some scientific knowledge and understanding. • Describe what the words objectivity, precision, accuracy, repeatability and reproducibility mean. • State how each of these would be ensured in your example investigation. • State why it is important to work scientifically. • Give one problem that could arise if investigations are not carried out scientifically. • Use some appropriate scientific words, symbols and units.

PROJECT 7: TEACHER NOTES
PROFESSION PORTFOLIO

NATIONAL CURRICULUM LINKS

Topics covered will depend on the careers researched.

WORKING SCIENTIFICALLY
Analysis and evaluation

CROSS-CURRICULAR OPPORTUNITIES INCLUDE:
- English – informative writing
- ICT – internet searching, word processing.

TIME

Three homework sessions of between 30 and 60 minutes each.

ADDITIONAL GUIDANCE

This task is designed to be completely open-ended and should allow students to research any career of interest to them which utilises any knowledge of science or requires similar skills to those used by scientists. Many students will believe that careers of interest to them may be completely unrelated to science and it is a good idea to have some examples to hand for these students. Examples include beauticians (biological knowledge of skin, chemical knowledge of electrolysis, etc.), plumbers (knowledge of behaviour of matter, i.e. water!), solicitors (analytical problem solving skills) – the list is endless!

ASSESSMENT, FEEDBACK AND IMPROVEMENT

Assessing these tasks should not be arduous. Rather than assigning an absolute grade, you should focus on how each student can improve. To ensure that this task is formative, students should be given the opportunity to improve their work based on the teacher's targets or through peer and self-assessment.

GUIDANCE FOR CONFIDENT (C)

Students working with confidence should be able to carry out an internet search, decide on careers to research and provide relevant information on these.

We find that reading through the project using these additional prompts helps to assess the task.

1

PROJECT 7: TASK SHEET (ESTABLISHING)
PROFESSION PORTFOLIO

If you choose to study science as you move through your school life, where might it take you?

Research jobs or careers of interest to you and find out ways science is useful in them, or how science is directly relevant to them.

Prepare a flier that can be used to inspire young people to take up a career in science.

This could be a specific career or a number of jobs related to the topic you are studying.

Use websites, magazines and books to get information to answer each section below. Use the ACE Learning Ladder to help you do your best.

Use your own words throughout the project.

SECTION 1: CAREERS OR JOBS YOU HAVE STUDIED
- Use the internet to find out about three jobs that interest you.
- What tasks would you do if you did these jobs?
- How do you get to do these jobs? Do you need certain qualifications for example?

SECTION 2: HOW IS SCIENCE RELEVANT TO THESE JOBS?
- How is science used in this job? List all the ways you think of or find out.
- Do you think any of the science topics you have studied would help in these jobs? Which ones?

SECTION 3: WHY ARE JOBS IN SCIENCE IMPORTANT?
- Find out what STEM means and why this is thought to be important.
- Explain why it is important for our country to have scientists.

Use the Good Project Guide sheet for tips on internet safety, research and literacy.

BIOLOGY HOMEWORK TASKS: TASK SHEET (ESTABLISHING)

PROJECT 7: TASK SHEET (CONFIDENT)
PROFESSION PORTFOLIO

If you choose to study science as you move through your school life, where might it take you? Will you just end up working in a science laboratory or teaching science? No!

Research jobs or careers of interest to you and find out ways science is useful in them, or how science is directly relevant to them.

Prepare a flier that can be used to inspire young people to take up a career in science.

This could be a specific career or a number of jobs related to the topic you are studying.

Use websites, magazines and books to get information to answer each section below. Use the ACE Learning Ladder to help you do your best.

Use your own words throughout the project.

SECTION 1: CAREERS OR JOBS YOU HAVE STUDIED
- Use the internet to find out about three jobs that interest you.
- Describe the duties of a person doing these jobs.
- Describe the qualifications a person would need to get these jobs.

SECTION 2: HOW IS SCIENCE RELEVANT TO THESE JOBS?
- List all the ways science may be relevant to these jobs.
- Decide which topics you have studied so far, if any, are similar to the science used in these jobs.

SECTION 3: WHY ARE JOBS IN SCIENCE IMPORTANT?
- Find out about the STEM agenda.
- Explain why it is important for our country to have scientists.

Use the Good Project Guide sheet for tips on internet safety, research and literacy.

BIOLOGY HOMEWORK TASKS: TASK SHEET (CONFIDENT)

If you choose to study science as you move through your school life, where might it take you?

Research jobs or careers of interest to you and find out ways science is useful in them, or how science is directly relevant to them.

Prepare a flier that can be used to inspire young people to take up a career in science.

This could be a specific career or a number of jobs related to the topic you are studying or any aspect of science you are interested in.

Use websites, magazines and books to get information to answer each section below. Use the ACE Learning Ladder to help you do your best.

Use your own words throughout the project.

You should cover the following in your flier:

SECTION 1: CAREERS OR JOBS YOU HAVE FOUND OUT ABOUT
- What jobs have you found out about? What do these jobs involve? How do you get these jobs?

SECTION 2: HOW IS SCIENCE RELEVANT TO THIS JOB?
- What aspects of science are used in the job? Do you need any science qualifications to do this job?

SECTION 3: WHY ARE JOBS IN SCIENCE AND OTHER 'STEM' SUBJECTS IMPORTANT?
- How do such jobs aid society or individual people? What other benefits do scientific careers have?

Use the Good Project Guide sheet for tips on internet safety, research and literacy.

BIOLOGY HOMEWORK TASKS: TASK SHEET (ADVANCED)

ACE LEARNING LADDER

Assessment Check	The types of things you can do:
Advanced	• Write a detailed flier, drawing on detailed scientific knowledge and understanding. • Describe job(s) in detail, explaining the types of roles involved, the qualifications and training required and the career pathways available. • Explain the parts of the job(s) that involve science, including the specific area of science, and those tasks which do not involve science. • Explain why STEM jobs are important for society and why STEM jobs are often not chosen as careers, using evidence to justify your comments. • Use a range of scientific words, symbols and units accurately.
Confident	• Write a flier, drawing on scientific knowledge and understanding. • Describe job(s) in detail, including what the job involves and the qualifications needed. • Explain how science is relevant to the job(s) discussed. • Explain why STEM jobs are important for society. • Use a range of appropriate scientific words, symbols and units.
Establishing	• Write a simple flier, drawing on some scientific knowledge and understanding. • Describe the typical tasks involved in the job(s). • Identify one or two ways that science may be relevant to the job(s). • State why science is important to society. • List one or two essential jobs that involve science. • Use some appropriate scientific words, symbols and units.

PROJECT 8: TEACHER NOTES
LIVING SCIENTISTS

NATIONAL CURRICULUM LINKS

This will depend on the scientist studied.

WORKING SCIENTIFICALLY
Scientific attitudes
Experimental skills and investigations
Analysis and evaluation
Measurement

TIME

Three homework sessions of between 30 and 60 minutes each.

ADDITIONAL GUIDANCE

Well-known scientists such as Richard Dawkins, Stephen Hawking, Heather Couper, David Attenborough, Susan Greenfield, Sue Blackmore, Robert Winston, James Watson, Jane Goodall, Craig Venter, James Lovelock, Yvonne Barr, Jocelyn Bell Burnell could be researched.

For less well-known scientists, we suggest going to university websites or charity or organisation websites such as the Institute of Physics, Royal Society of Chemistry, Society of Biology or Cancer Research UK.

Learners may know a scientist and want to interview them or they may know of a famous scientist that they would like to find out about.

ASSESSMENT, FEEDBACK AND IMPROVEMENT

Assessing these tasks should not be arduous. Rather than assigning an absolute grade, you should focus on how each student can improve. To ensure that this task is formative, students should be given the opportunity to improve their work based on the teacher's targets or through peer and self-assessment.

GUIDANCE FOR CONFIDENT (C)

Students who are working with confidence should be able to carry out an internet search, decide on a scientist and recognise which area of science that person works in. The student should be able to describe why the scientist's work is important.

1 PROJECT 8: TASK SHEET (ESTABLISHING)
LIVING SCIENTISTS

There are thousands of scientists working in Britain and many more around the world. Use the internet to find out about the work of a living scientist. A lot of scientists have web pages about their work that you can read.

You have been asked to write a biography (life story) of a living scientist for a popular science magazine and write about what sort of scientist you would like to be.

Your teacher will tell you when to do each section.

Use websites, magazines and books to get information to answer each section below. Use the ACE Learning Ladder to help you do your best.

Use your own words throughout the project.

SECTION 1: RESEARCH AND DECIDE ON A LIVING SCIENTIST
- Use the internet to find out about a several scientists and what they do.
- Choose one scientist who you want to write about.
- Describe how you went about doing your research.
- Explain why you chose this scientist.

SECTION 2: LIFE OF A LIVING SCIENTIST
Write a biography of the living scientist you have chosen.
- Write about the scientist – include their name, where they work and interesting information.
- Describe the scientist's job. Who do they work for? Who do they work with?
- Explain why the scientist's work is important – for example will their work help certain people?

SECTION 3: YOUR LIFE AS A SCIENTIST
- If you had to be a scientist, what type of job would you do?
- Write a short story, draw a cartoon or make a short PowerPoint about your life as a scientist.

Use the Good Project Guide sheet for tips on internet safety, research and literacy.

BIOLOGY HOMEWORK TASKS: TASK SHEET (ESTABLISHING)

1

PROJECT 8: TASK SHEET (CONFIDENT)
LIVING SCIENTISTS

There are thousands of scientists working in Britain and many more around the world. Use the internet to find out about the work of a scientist. A lot of scientists have web pages about their work that you can read.

You are to write a biography (life story) of a living scientist and also write about what sort of scientist you would like to be. You may know a scientist you could interview or you may know of a famous scientist you would like to find out about. Either is fine, but carry out an internet search as well.

Your teacher will tell you when to do each section.

Use websites, magazines and books to get information to answer each section below. Use the ACE Learning Ladder to help you do your best.

Use your own words throughout the project.

SECTION 1: RESEARCH AND DECIDE ON A LIVING SCIENTIST
- Use the internet to find out about a range of scientists and what they do.
- Choose one scientist who you want to write about.
- Describe how you went about doing your research.
- Explain why you chose this scientist.

SECTION 2: LIFE OF A LIVING SCIENTIST
- Write a biography of the living scientist you have chosen.
- Write about the scientist – include their name, where they work and interesting information.
- Describe the scientist's job. Who do they work for? Who do they work with?
- Explain why the scientist's work is important.

SECTION 3: YOUR LIFE AS A SCIENTIST
- If you had to be a scientist, what type of job would you do?
- Write a short story, draw a cartoon or make a short PowerPoint about your life as a scientist.

Use the Good Project Guide sheet for tips on internet safety, research and literacy.

BIOLOGY HOMEWORK TASKS: TASK SHEET (CONFIDENT)

There are thousands of scientists working in Britain and many more around the world. Use the internet to find out about the work of a scientist. A lot of scientists have web pages about their work that you can read.

You are to write a biography (life story) of a living scientist and also write about what sort of scientist you would like to be. You may know a scientist you could interview or you may know of a famous scientist you would like to find out about. Either is fine, but carry out an internet search as well.

Your teacher will tell you when to do each section.

Use websites, magazines and books to get information to answer each section below. Use the ACE Learning Ladder to help you do your best.

Use your own words throughout the project.

SECTION 1: RESEARCH AND DECIDE ON A LIVING SCIENTIST
- Research several scientists and their work.
- Explain which scientist you have chosen and why.
- Explain how you conducted your research.

SECTION 2: LIFE OF A LIVING SCIENTIST
- Write a detailed biography of the living scientist you have chosen.
- Include information about the work they have carried out and why it is important to the wider world.

SECTION 3: YOUR LIFE AS A SCIENTIST
- If you had to be a scientist, what type of job would you do?
- Write a short story, draw a cartoon or make a short PowerPoint about your life as a scientist.

Use the Good Project Guide sheet for tips on internet safety, research and literacy.

BIOLOGY HOMEWORK TASKS: TASK SHEET (ADVANCED)

PROJECT 8: ACE LEARNING LADDER
LIVING SCIENTISTS

ACE LEARNING LADDER

Assessment Check	The types of things you can do:
Advanced	• Write a comprehensive biography about a living scientist. • Consider the ethical, moral and financial implications of the scientist's work, making your own judgement about its value. • Explain how the scientist would ensure that their work is valid and reliable. • Give a detailed explanation on how your own scientific work could be of value to society as a whole and influenced by society.
Confident	• Write a detailed biography about a living scientist. • Explain how society may be affected by the scientist's research. • Link the scientist's work/research to underpinning scientific ideas, and describe the scientific methods the scientist would follow. • Discuss the impact your life as a scientist could have on society. • Identify a science-related job you could do and explain the reasons for your choice.
Establishing	• Write a basic bibliography on a living scientist. • Identify one or two pieces of scientific information the scientist has found out or researched. • Identify the main area of science the scientist works in. • Suggest a scientific job you would like to do, giving a reason for your choice.

NATIONAL CURRICULUM LINKS

CELLS AND ORGANISATION

- cells as the fundamental unit of living organisms, including how to observe, interpret and record cell structure using a light microscope
- the functions of the cell wall, cell membrane, cytoplasm, nucleus, vacuole, mitochondria and chloroplasts
- the similarities and differences between plant and animal cells.

WORKING SCIENTIFICALLY
Experimental skills and investigations

TIME

Three homework sessions of between 30 and 60 minutes each, depending on ability.

ADDITIONAL GUIDANCE

Students will need to have learnt the main cell organelles (cell wall, cell membrane, cytoplasm, nucleus, vacuole, mitochondria and chloroplasts) and should be able to give descriptions of the role of each. They must have used a light microscope to observe cells before completing this homework task. Students working towards or at Advanced (A) level should be familiar with the different magnifications available on light microscopes and know how these may influence what is seen when tissues are observed. Advanced students should also be guided to resources about electron microscopes so they can consider the different capabilities and working of these.

ASSESSMENT, FEEDBACK AND IMPROVEMENT

Assessing these tasks should not be arduous. Rather than assigning an absolute grade, you should focus on how each student can improve. To ensure that this task is formative, students should be given the opportunity to improve their work based on the teacher's targets or through peer and self-assessment.

GUIDANCE FOR CONFIDENT (C)

Students working with confidence will be able to carry out any relevant internet searches, give a detailed description of how to use a microscope (not how it works internally) and explain why some cell organelles will be visible under a light microscope whereas others will not, and explain the role of most organelles.
We find that reading through the project using these additional prompts helps to assess the task.

2 MAKING AND PRESENTING 1: TASK SHEET (ESTABLISHING)
MARVELLOUS MICROSCOPES

Scientists have been able to learn a great deal about cells by using microscopes. Microscopes allow structures that are usually invisible to us to be seen. Microscopes work by enlarging, or 'magnifying' images using lenses. You will have used light microscopes in your lessons to observe some cells.

Write a handy guide on how to use light microscopes. Include information about the parts of a cell that you may see.

Use websites, magazines and books to get information to answer each section below. Use the ACE Learning Ladder to help you do your best.

Use your own words throughout the project.

SECTION 1: HOW TO USE A LIGHT MICROSCOPE
- Include a labelled diagram of a microscope, explaining what each part does.
- Describe how to prepare a slide.
- Describe how to focus the microscope.

SECTION 2: HOW TO RECORD IMAGES
- Include an example of a cell observed under a microscope.
- Describe what information to include on diagrams.
- Describe what to draw the image with and how big to draw it.

SECTION 3: WHAT YOU MAY OBSERVE
- Include a labelled diagram of a plant cell and an animal cell.
- Describe what each part of the cell does.
- Describe why only some parts may be seen under the microscope.

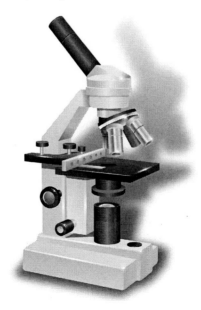

Use the Good Project Guide sheet for tips on internet safety, research and literacy.

Scientists have been able to learn a great deal about cells by using microscopes. They allow structures that are usually invisible to us to be seen. Microscopes work by enlarging, or 'magnifying' images using lenses. You will have used light microscopes in your lessons to observe some cells.

Write a handy guide on how to use light microscopes. Include information about the parts of a cell that you may see.

Use websites, magazines and books to get information to answer each section below. Use the ACE Learning Ladder to help you do your best.

Use your own words throughout the project.

SECTION 1: HOW TO USE A LIGHT MICROSCOPE
- Include a labelled diagram of a microscope, explaining what each part does.
- Describe how to prepare a slide.
- Describe how to focus the microscope.

SECTION 2: HOW TO RECORD IMAGES
- Include an example of a cell observed under a microscope.
- Describe what information to include on diagrams.
- Describe what to draw the image with and how big to draw it.

SECTION 3: WHAT YOU MAY OBSERVE
- Include a labelled diagram of a plant cell and an animal cell.
- Describe what each part of the cell does.
- Describe why only some parts may be seen under the microscope.

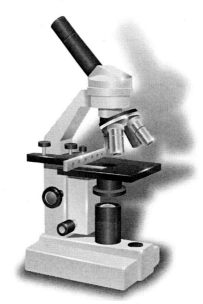

Use the Good Project Guide sheet for tips on internet safety, research and literacy.

Scientists have been able to learn a great deal about cells by using microscopes. They allow structures that are usually invisible to us to be seen. Microscopes work by enlarging, or 'magnifying' images using lenses. You will have used light microscopes in your lessons to observe some cells.

Write a handy guide on how to use light microscopes. Include information about the parts of a cell that you may see.

Use websites, magazines and books to get information to answer each section below. Use the ACE Learning Ladder to help you do your best.

Use your own words throughout the project.

SECTION 1: HOW TO USE A LIGHT MICROSCOPE
- Include a labelled diagram of a microscope, explaining what each part does.
- Describe how to prepare a slide.
- Describe how to focus the microscope.
- Include an example of a cell observed under a microscope. Explain what needs to be included with diagrams of observed cells.

SECTION 2: WHAT YOU MAY OBSERVE
- Include a labelled diagram of a plant cell and an animal cell.
- Describe what each part of the cell does.
- Describe why only some parts may be seen under the microscope.
- Explain how the magnification affects what you may observe.

SECTION 3: TYPES OF MICROSCOPE
- Find out what an electron microscope is.
- Explain what the main differences are between light microscopes and electron microscopes.
- Suggest when each type of microscope may be used.

Use the Good Project Guide sheet for tips on internet safety, research and literacy.

ACE LEARNING LADDER

Assessment Check	The types of things you can do:
Advanced	• Explain how to use a light microscope and how to record observations in detail, drawing on detailed scientific knowledge and understanding. • Discuss why only some cell parts can be observed, in terms of the magnification of the light microscope. • Compare what can be observed using light microscopes and electron microscopes. • Suggest when each type of microscope would be used based on scientific understanding. • Compare, in detail, the structures found in animal and plant cells. • Use a range of scientific words, symbols and units accurately.
Confident	• Explain how to use a light microscope and how to record observations in detail, drawing on scientific knowledge and understanding. • Explain why only some cell parts can be seen. • Describe the key information to include on diagrams of observed cells. • Explain the role of the main parts of cells. • Compare the cell parts seen in plant and animal cells. • Use a range of appropriate scientific words, symbols and units.
Establishing	• Describe, simply, how to use a light microscope, drawing on some scientific knowledge and understanding. • Describe the steps you carry out when using a light microscope. • Give an example of a labelled diagram of an observed cell and describe what should be included in the diagram. • Label a picture of a plant cell and an animal cell. • Use some appropriate scientific words, symbols and units.

NATIONAL CURRICULUM LINKS

RELATIONSHIPS IN AN ECOSYSTEM
- the interdependence of organisms in an ecosystem, including food webs and insect pollinated crops.

PHOTOSYNTHESIS
- the reactants in, and products of, photosynthesis, and a word summary for photosynthesis
- the dependence of almost all life on Earth on the ability of photosynthetic organisms, such as plants and algae, to use sunlight in photosynthesis to build organic molecules that are an essential energy store and to maintain levels of oxygen and carbon dioxide in the atmosphere
- the adaptations of leaves for photosynthesis.

WORKING SCIENTIFICALLY
Analysis and evaluation

CROSS-CURRICULAR OPPORTUNITIES INCLUDE:
- art – illustrations/images of plants.

TIME

Three homework sessions of between 30 and 60 minutes each, depending on ability.

ADDITIONAL GUIDANCE

This task will allow students to study the plant life in their local area. It is hoped that it will allow students to become more familiar with plant life, for example by identifying types of trees and also develop their ability to classify species. Students will need to be familiar with some plant classification before attempting this task. You may wish to spend a lesson looking at a variety of plants (or leaf samples from trees) and deciding on how different groups are classified.

ASSESSMENT, FEEDBACK AND IMPROVEMENT

Assessing these tasks should not be arduous. Rather than assigning an absolute grade, you should focus on how each student can improve. To ensure that this task is formative, students should be given the opportunity to improve their work based on the teacher's targets or through peer and self-assessment.

GUIDANCE FOR CONFIDENT (C)

Students working with confidence will demonstrate an understanding of the relationship between the structure and function of parts of a plant.

We find that reading through the project using these additional prompts helps to assess the task.

There are so many species of plants around us, so how can you tell what they all are?

Are there clues that make recognising plants easier, or clever ways to remember their names?

Prepare a guidebook on the local area's plant life which tourists could use as a quick way of finding out about the various species they may see.
- Select at least three examples of plants to include in your guide.
- Give the name of each plant and make a diagram or take a photograph of it.
- Include ways to identify each plant, e.g. the shape of the leaf or the colour of the bark.
- Give any interesting or useful information about the species you have chosen.

Use websites, magazines and books to get information. Use the ACE Learning Ladder to help you do your best.

Use your own words throughout the project.

Use the Good Project Guide sheet for tips on internet safety, research and literacy.

There are so many species of plants around us, so how can you tell what they all are?

Are there clues that make recognising plants easier, or clever ways to remember their names?

Prepare a guidebook on the local area's plant life which tourists could use as a quick way of finding out about the various species they may see.
- Select at least five examples of plants to include in your guide.
- Give the name of each plant and make a diagram or take a photograph of it.
- Include ways to identify each plant, e.g. the shape of the leaf or the colour of the bark.
- Try and include information on the family of plants each species belongs to.
- Give any interesting or useful information about the species you have chosen.

Use websites, magazines and books to get information. Use the ACE Learning Ladder to help you do your best.

Use your own words throughout the project.

Use the Good Project Guide sheet for tips on internet safety, research and literacy.

There are so many species of plants around us, so how can you tell what they all are?

Are there clues that make recognising plants easier, or clever ways to remember their names?

Prepare a guidebook on the local area's plant life which tourists could use as a quick way of finding out about the various species they may see.

Choose one type of plant e.g. trees, grasses, flowering plants (daises, buttercups or others).
• Select at least 10 examples of your selected plant type to include in your guide.
• Give the name of each plant and make a detailed diagram or photograph of it.
• Include ways to identify each plant, e.g. the shape of the leaf or the colour of the bark.
• Include information on the family of plants the species belong to.
• Give any interesting or useful information about the species you have chosen.

Use websites, magazines and books to get information. Use the ACE Learning Ladder to help you do your best.

Use your own words throughout the project.

Use the Good Project Guide sheet for tips on internet safety, research and literacy.

2

ACE LEARNING LADDER

Assessment Check	The types of things you can do:
Advanced	• Prepare a detailed guidebook, drawing on detailed scientific knowledge and understanding. • Explain the key identification points of at least 10 plants. • Explain the similarities and differences between the plants in terms of the reproduction, photosynthesis and cells present. • Develop a detailed key to identify all your plants. • Explain the significance of the plants within the local habitat and to the wider environment. • Use a range of scientific words, symbols and units accurately.
Confident	• Prepare a guidebook, drawing on scientific knowledge and understanding. • Explain the key identification points of at least 5 plants. • Explain the similarities and differences between the plants, in terms of how they photosynthesise and reproduce and disperse seeds for example. • Develop a key to identify all your plants. • Explain how the plants are useful to people or the environment. • Use a range of appropriate scientific words, symbols and units.
Establishing	• Make a simple guidebook, drawing on some scientific knowledge and understanding. • Describe the appearance of at least three different plants, using appropriate drawings or images. • State key differences between the plants that could be used to identify them. • Draw a simple key to identify the plants. • Give one interesting fact about one of the plants. • Use some appropriate scientific words, symbols and units.

NATIONAL CURRICULUM LINKS

RELATIONSHIPS IN AN ECOSYSTEM
- the interdependence of organisms in an ecosystem, including food webs and insect pollinated crops
- how organisms affect, and are affected by, their environment, including the accumulation of toxic materials.

WORKING SCIENTIFICALLY
Experimental skills and investigations
Analysis and evaluation

CROSS–CURRICULAR OPPORTUNITIES INCLUDE:
- geography – knowledge of chosen animals' surroundings.

TIME

Three homework sessions of between 30 and 60 minutes each, depending on ability.

ADDITIONAL GUIDANCE

Students should be familiar with the life processes that all living things share, habitats and adaptation. Students will need to spend a little bit of time getting used to making observations about animals before trying to complete this task. This could be done as a class practical looking at insects or by a visit to a zoo for example. Explain to students that, although their storyboard is to be made up by them, and they can include any events they wish, it should be a reflection of how the chosen animal does behave. One option when setting this task is to study an animal as a class, perhaps through watching a wildlife documentary and then carrying out further research. All students could then be asked to design their storyboard about the same animal.

ASSESSMENT, FEEDBACK AND IMPROVEMENT

Assessing these tasks should not be arduous. Rather than assigning an absolute grade, you should focus on how each student can improve. To ensure that this task is formative, students should be given the opportunity to improve their work based on the teacher's targets or through peer and self-assessment.

GUIDANCE FOR CONFIDENT (C)

Students working with confidence will be able to discuss the animal's habitat and adaptations and discuss the mains issues of threats and conservation.

Millions of animals live on Earth and they all behave in unique ways. You may have watched wildlife programmes about certain animals. These shows tell us what animals are like, where they live and what their lives are like from day to day.

Imagine you are a wildlife expert and have been observing a family of animals for the past year. Plan a programme to tell everyone what you have found out.

Research an animal of your choice (you could use books, television programmes, the internet or you could observe real animals).

Design a storyboard (a series of pictures with descriptions of what the presenter would talk about in the real programme) which shows what has happened to your animals across the year. You should base this on your research.

Divide your storyboard into 12 sections, one for each month of the year. Describe what happens to your animals across the year, giving reasons for why the animals behave as they do.

Helpful tips:
- Your storyboard will be fictional, but the events you make up should be very close to the real behaviour of your animals.
- Make sure you describe how your animals interact with other wildlife.
- Include what their habitat is like and how they use it.

Use the ACE Learning Ladder to help you do your best.

Use your own words throughout the project.

Use the Good Project Guide sheet for tips on internet safety, research and literacy.

BIOLOGY HOMEWORK TASKS: TASK SHEET (ESTABLISHING)

Millions of animals live on Earth and they all behave in unique ways. You may have watched wildlife programmes about certain animals. These shows tell us what animals are like, where they live and what their lives are like from day to day.

Imagine you are a wildlife expert and have been observing a family of animals for the past year. Plan a programme to tell every one what you have found out.

Research an animal of your choice.

Design a storyboard (a series of pictures with descriptions of what the presenter would talk about in the real programme) showing what has happened to your animals across the year.

Include detailed descriptions of what happens to your animals across the year, giving reasons for why the animals behave as they do.

Tips:
- Your storyboard will be fictional, but the events you make up should reflect the real behaviour of your animals.
- Make sure you describe how your animals interact with other wildlife and their habitat.

Use the ACE Learning Ladder to help you do your best.

Use your own words throughout the project.

Use the Good Project Guide sheet for tips on internet safety, research and literacy.

Millions of animals live on Earth and they all behave in unique ways. You may have watched wildlife programmes about certain animals. These shows tell us what animals are like, where they live and what their lives are like from day to day.

Imagine you are a wildlife expert and have been observing a family of animals for the past year. Plan a programme to tell every one what you have found out. Set out a storyboard showing what footage of the animals you will show and what commentary you will give through the scenes.

- Research an animal of your choice.
- Use your storyboard to show your audience what a typical year would be like for your animal.

Use the ACE Learning Ladder to help you do your best.

Use your own words throughout the project.

Use the Good Project Guide sheet for tips on internet safety, research and literacy.

ACE LEARNING LADDER

Assessment Check	The types of things you can do:
Advanced	• Produce a detailed storyboard, drawing on detailed scientific knowledge and understanding. • Explain how the animal behaves across the year, using food chains, food webs and pyramids of biomass to describe its feeding relationships. • Explain how the animal is adapted to its environment, how subsequent generations may or may not show changes in characteristics and how such changes are a part of natural selection over many generations. • Explain how the population of the animal changes across the year and how the global population is likely to change across the year and in the future. • Explain how external influences will affect the animal's population. • Use a range of scientific words and symbols accurately.
Confident	• Produce a storyboard, drawing on scientific knowledge and understanding. • Explain how the animal behaves across the year, using food chains and webs to describe its feeding relationships. • Explain how the animal is adapted to its environment, and how subsequent generations may or may not show changes in characteristics. • Explain how the population of the animal changes across the year. • Consider how the population is affected by changes in the habitat. • Use a range of appropriate scientific words and symbols.
Establishing	• Produce a simple storyboard, drawing on some scientific knowledge and understanding. • State some events that happen to the animal across the year. • Identify one or two adaptations the animal exhibits. • Describe how the numbers of the animal change across the year. • List one or two factors that could affect the animal's population. • Use some appropriate scientific words and symbols.

NATIONAL CURRICULUM LINKS

The topics covered will depend on the discoveries chosen.

WORKING SCIENTIFICALLY
Scientific attitudes
Analysis and evaluation

CROSS-CURRICULAR OPPORTUNITIES INCLUDE:
*   history – use of sources for research.

TIME

Three homework sessions of between 30 and 60 minutes each, depending on ability.

ADDITIONAL GUIDANCE

This is a very open-ended task and should require little scientific knowledge and understanding to complete. It will give students an opportunity to research scientific discoveries and consider if any are more significant in comparison to others. Obviously there is a plethora of discoveries and developments for students to think about so it may be advisable, especially for lower ability classes, to help narrow down their research, perhaps by giving a list of 10–20 discoveries of your choosing and a brief synopsis from which they can then carry out their own research.

ASSESSMENT, FEEDBACK AND IMPROVEMENT

Assessing these tasks should not be arduous. Rather than assigning an absolute grade, you should focus on how each student can improve. To ensure that this task is formative, students should be given the opportunity to improve their work based on the teacher's targets or through peer and self-assessment.

GUIDANCE FOR CONFIDENT (C)

Students working with confidence will make a coherent and detailed timeline.

We find that reading through the project using these additional prompts helps to assess the task.

MAKING AND PRESENTING 4: TASK SHEET (ESTABLISHING)
SCIENCE TIMELINE

Humans have always been fascinated by the world around them and this has led to science being present in even the earliest human populations (although they may not have called it science!). So what are the most important discoveries and developments that have occurred in science? When and why did they happen?

Choose major scientific or technological developments you think are important.

Design a timeline showing key scientific discoveries in the order in which they happened.
- Try and include at least five key discoveries in your timeline.
- Give an approximate date for the discoveries.
- Describe why each discovery was important.
- Include illustrations or pictures in your timeline.

Use websites, magazines and books to get information. Use the ACE Learning Ladder to help you do your best.

Use your own words throughout the project.

Tips and ideas
Make a timeline like a washing line and peg your events along it.

Use the Good Project Guide sheet for tips on internet safety, research and literacy.

BIOLOGY HOMEWORK TASKS: TASK SHEET (ESTABLISHING)

SCIENCE TIMELINE

Humans have always been fascinated by the world around them and this has led to science being present in even the earliest human populations (although they may not have called it science!). So what are the most important discoveries and developments that have occurred in science? When and why did they happen?

Choose major scientific or technological developments you think are important.

Design a timeline showing key scientific discoveries in the order in which they happened.
- Try and include 10 to 15 key discoveries in your timeline.
- Give an approximate date and description of the discoveries.
- Describe why each discovery was important.
- Include illustrations or pictures in your timeline.

Use websites, magazines and books to get information. Use the ACE Learning Ladder to help you do your best.

Use your own words throughout the project.

Use the Good Project Guide sheet for tips on internet safety, research and literacy.

BIOLOGY HOMEWORK TASKS: TASK SHEET (CONFIDENT)

Humans have always been fascinated by the world around them and this has led to science being present in even the earliest human populations (although they may not have called it science!). So what are the most important discoveries and developments that have occurred in science? When and why did they happen?

Choose major scientific or technological developments you think are important.

Design a timeline showing key scientific discoveries in the order in which they happened.
- Try and include a minimum of 15 key discoveries in your timeline.
- Include relevant dates, people and places.
- Explain in detail why each discovery was important.
- Consider the impact on society and the influences from society that led to each discovery.
- Include illustrations or pictures in your timeline.

Use websites, magazines and books to get information. Use the ACE Learning Ladder to help you do your best.

Use your own words throughout the project.

Use the Good Project Guide sheet for tips on internet safety, research and literacy.

ACE LEARNING LADDER

Assessment Check	The types of things you can do:
Advanced	• Produce a detailed timeline drawing on detailed scientific knowledge and understanding. • Place discoveries in date order, giving detailed accounts of who made the discovery and when and how they made it. • Explain what scientific principles underpin the discoveries and why some discoveries could not have been made earlier, in terms of knowledge or technology available. • Explain how the knowledge about each discovery has progressed since the discovery, and how new discoveries confirmed or challenged it. • Explain how the discovery has positively and negatively impacted on society and the wider scientific world. • Use a range of scientific words accurately.
Confident	• Produce a timeline, drawing on scientific knowledge and understanding. • Place discoveries in date order, giving the name of the scientist who made the discovery and when and how they made it. • Link each discovery to the scientific principles that it relates to. • Explain how the knowledge about the discovery has progressed since the discovery. • Explain how the discovery has impacted on society and the wider scientific world. • Use a range of appropriate scientific words.
Establishing	• Draw or make a simple timeline, using some of your scientific knowledge and understanding. • Make a timeline with details of what discoveries were made, when and by whom. • Identify the major branch of science each discovery links to. • State some consequences of the discoveries. • Use some appropriate scientific words.

NATIONAL CURRICULUM LINKS

The task can fit with any topic, depending on the subject of the script.

WORKING SCIENTIFICALLY
Scientific attitudes
Analysis and evaluation

CROSS–CURRICULAR OPPORTUNITIES INCLUDE:

- English – scriptwriting.

TIME

Three homework sessions of between 30 and 60 minutes each, depending on ability.

ASSESSMENT, FEEDBACK AND IMPROVEMENT

Assessing these tasks should not be arduous. Rather than assigning an absolute grade, you should focus on how each student can improve. To ensure that this task is formative, students should be given the opportunity to improve their work based on the teacher's targets or through peer and self-assessment.

GUIDANCE FOR CONFIDENT (C)

Students working with confidence will demonstrate an understanding of the issue, using scientific knowledge and terms to explain the concepts or arguments.

We find that reading through the project using these additional prompts helps to assess the task.

SCIENTIFIC SCRIPTWRITING

Whenever you look at a newspaper or turn on the television you will see reports on problems around the world. Often these involve science – endangered animals or global warming, for example. So how can people be made aware of these issues and of what they can do to tackle them?

- Research a scientific issue that interests you.
- Write a script for a short television news item (no more than a couple of minutes) explaining to viewers all about the problem you have chosen.
- Your script should include any relevant scientific facts, drawings or photographs and any important information.

Tips
- Use television, newspapers, books or the internet to help you choose a topic that interests you.
- Decide what information you will need to include in your script to get your viewers' attention and interest.
- Make sure you use your knowledge of science to help describe the issue.

Use the ACE Learning Ladder to help you do your best.

Use your own words throughout the project.

Use the Good Project Guide sheet for tips on internet safety, research and literacy.

SCIENTIFIC SCRIPTWRITING

Whenever you look at a newspaper or turn on the television you will see reports on problems around the world. Often these involve science – endangered animals or global warming, for example. So how can people be made aware of these issues and of what they can do to tackle them?

- Research a scientific issue that interests you.
- Write a script for a short television bulletin or appeal (no more than 3 minutes) all about the issue.
- Include any relevant scientific facts, drawings or photographs.

Tips
- Decide what information you will need to include in your script and the best way to set it out.
- Make sure you use your knowledge of science to help describe the issue.

Use the ACE Learning Ladder to help you do your best.

Use your own words throughout the project.

Use the Good Project Guide sheet for tips on internet safety, research and literacy.

Whenever you look at a newspaper or turn on the television you will see reports on problems around the world. Often these involve science – endangered animals or global warming, for example. So how can people be made aware of these issues and of what they can do to tackle them?

- Research a scientific issue which interests you and prepare a script for a short television news item (a 3-minute bulletin) all about the issue.
- Explain scientific ideas about your issue of choice in detail, in easy to understand language.
- Give different points of view about the issue.
- Use evidence or statistics for the points that you include in your report.

Use the ACE Learning Ladder to help you do your best.

Use your own words throughout the project.

Use the Good Project Guide sheet for tips on internet safety, research and literacy.

ACE LEARNING LADDER

Assessment Check	The types of things you can do:
Advanced	• Write a detailed scientific script, drawing on detailed scientific knowledge and understanding. • Explain, accurately, the issue your script is about, referring to the underlying scientific principles, and say how it fits with current scientific research. • Explain the different viewpoints people have about the scientific issue, classifying whether these are fact, opinion or speculation. • Explain whether or not the scientific issue is beneficial to the wider world, using evidence to justify your decision. • Explain how you have ensured your script gives a balanced viewpoint on the issue. • Use a range of scientific words, symbols and units accurately.
Confident	• Write a scientific script, drawing on scientific knowledge and understanding. • Explain, accurately, the issue your script is about, referring to the underlying scientific principles. • Explain the different viewpoints people have about the scientific issue. • Explain how the scientific issue in your script impacts on society or the environment. • Refer to several pieces of evidence about the issue within your script. • Use a range of appropriate scientific words, symbols and units.
Establishing	• Write a simple script, drawing on some scientific knowledge and understanding. • Describe the area of science your script is about. • State one or two viewpoints people have about the issue your script is about. • Describe whether you think the issue your script is about is good or bad, giving a simple reason. • Use some appropriate scientific words, symbols and units.

MAKING AND PRESENTING 6: TEACHER NOTES
SCINTILLATING SCIENCE!

NATIONAL CURRICULUM LINKS

This will depend on the focus chosen by students:

WORKING SCIENTIFICALLY
Scientific attitudes
Experimental skills and investigations
Analysis and evaluation

CROSS–CURRICULAR OPPORTUNITIES INCLUDE:
- English – genres of writing and creative writing
- ICT – internet searching, word processing
- art – design of leaflet.

TIME

Three homework sessions of between 30 and 60 minutes each, depending on ability.

ADDITIONAL GUIDANCE

Students need very little scientific knowledge to be able to complete this task. The task would be ideal for students who are just beginning their studies at Key Stage 3.

A good way to introduce the task could be to first discuss what students feel science is and then look through university brochures or a school brochure to see how each subject area sells itself and the descriptions they give of their topic. You could also look up the definition of science in the dictionary and discuss as a class what opinions they have on this.

ASSESSMENT, FEEDBACK AND IMPROVEMENT

Assessing these tasks should not be arduous. Rather than assigning an absolute grade, you should focus on how each student can improve. To ensure that this task is formative, students should be given the opportunity to improve their work based on the teacher's targets or through peer and self-assessment.

GUIDANCE FOR CONFIDENT (C)

Students working with confidence will be able to present ideas about science being experimental and the key ideas (energy, forces, particles and cells). They should recognise a number of different types of scientist, e.g. astronauts, doctors, ecologists.

We find that reading through the project using these additional prompts helps to assess the task.

Imagine if an alien from outer space landed on Earth and didn't know anything about science! They wouldn't know what you could learn in science lessons or what scientists in the past have discovered or all the amazing things about science.

Use websites, magazines and books to make a leaflet to give to the alien which explains all about 'science'.

Make your leaflet informative but easy to use; you don't want to put the alien off reading it!

Include any pictures or facts that you think would help explain what science is.

Ideas to think about:
- What photos or drawings could help to show what science is all about?
- Explain what science is.
- Describe the types of jobs scientists do.
- Explain why science is important, for example to people, animals, the planet...

Use websites, magazines and books to get information.
Use the ACE Learning Ladder to help you do your best.

Use your own words throughout the project.

Use the Good Project Guide sheet for tips on internet safety, research and literacy.

Imagine if an alien from outer space landed on Earth and didn't know anything about science! They wouldn't know what you could learn in science lessons or what scientists in the past have discovered or all the amazing things about science.

Use websites, magazines and books to make a leaflet to give to the alien which explains all about 'science'.

Make your leaflet informative but easy to use; you don't want to put the alien off reading it!

Include any pictures or facts that you think would help explain what science is. Ideas to think about:
- What images help to show what science is about?
- Explain what science is.
- Describe what scientists do.
- Explain why science is important.

Use websites, magazines and books to get information.
Use the ACE Learning Ladder to help you do your best.

Use your own words throughout the project.

Use the Good Project Guide sheet for tips on internet safety, research and literacy.

Imagine if an alien from outer space landed on Earth and didn't know anything about science! They wouldn't know what you could learn in science lessons or what scientists in the past have discovered or all the amazing things about science.

Use websites, magazines and books to make a leaflet to give to the alien which explains all about 'science'.

Make your leaflet informative but easy to use; you don't want to put the alien off reading it!

It is up to you how you make your leaflet informative; however, you should make sure you include pictures, facts and discussions on what scientists do and why science is important.

Use websites, magazines and books to get information. Use the ACE Learning Ladder to help you do your best.

Use your own words throughout the project.

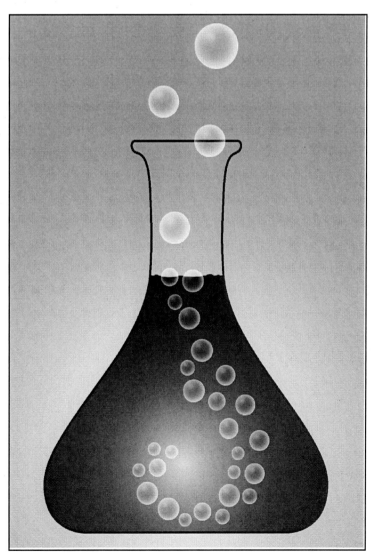

Use the Good Project Guide sheet for tips on internet safety, research and literacy.

2 MAKING AND PRESENTING 6: ACE LEARNING LADDER
SCINTILLATING SCIENCE!

ACE LEARNING LADDER

Assessment Check	The types of things you can do:
Advanced	• Make a detailed leaflet about what science is, drawing on detailed scientific knowledge and understanding. • Compare the roles of different scientists, discussing the specialisms they work in. • Justify why science is important, using evidence to support your views. • Explain how science has affected society, both positively and negatively. • Explain how scientific discoveries have changed worldviews or have had unexpected consequences. • Use a range of scientific words, symbols and units accurately.
Confident	• Make a leaflet about what science is, drawing on scientific knowledge and understanding. • Explain, simply, what scientists do. • Explain why science is important. • Explain how science has affected society. • Describe how aspects of science are applied in particular jobs or roles. • Use a range of appropriate scientific words, symbols and units.
Establishing	• Make a simple leaflet about what science is, drawing on some scientific knowledge and understanding. • State what scientists do. • State why science is important. • Name one or two scientific discoveries. • Name some apparatus or knowledge a scientist may need to use. • Use some appropriate scientific words, symbols and units.

NATIONAL CURRICULUM LINKS

RELATIONSHIPS IN AN ECOSYSTEM
- the interdependence of organisms in an ecosystem, including food webs and insect pollinated crops.

WORKING SCIENTIFICALLY
Scientific attitudes
Experimental skills and investigations
Analysis and evaluation
Measurement

CROSS–CURRICULAR OPPORTUNITIES INCLUDE:
- mathematics – recording data
- art – drawing organisms.

TIME

Three homework sessions of between 30 and 60 minutes each, depending on ability.

ASSESSMENT, FEEDBACK AND IMPROVEMENT

Assessing these tasks should not be arduous. Rather than assigning an absolute grade, you should focus on how each student can improve. To ensure that this task is formative, students should be given the opportunity to improve their work based on the teacher's targets or through peer and self-assessment.

GUIDANCE FOR CONFIDENT (C)

Students working with confidence choose a fair, reliable method to count organisms and make conclusions based on their results.

We find that reading through the project using these additional prompts helps to assess the task.

3 MINI INVESTIGATION 1: TASK SHEET (ESTABLISHING)
COUNTING CREATURES

Living creatures are all around us. You may think there isn't any wildlife in your back garden, but there are probably hundreds of creatures right under your nose!

You are going to choose a living creature to investigate and try to find out how many live in your garden or local park and how their behaviour and numbers change over a month.

1. Pick a creature you wish to study. Pick something you will be able to find easily, e.g. woodlice, spiders, robins.
2. Devise a way to work out the population of the animal.
3. Monitor the population over a month (choose how many times you would like to check the population) and record and explain any changes you notice.

Use the ACE Learning Ladder to help you do your best.

Use your own words throughout the project.

Use the Good Project Guide sheet for tips on internet safety, research and literacy.

RESEARCH TIPS
When you research, follow these tips:
- How will you choose the creature you will monitor?
- How will you recognise and identify it?
- How will you calculate the population? Remember you won't be able to count every single organism.
- How will you record your data?
- How often will you need to record the organism's numbers to be able to look for patterns?

Living creatures are all around us. You may think there isn't any wildlife in your back garden, but there are probably hundreds of creatures right under your nose!

You are going to choose a living creature to investigate and try to find out how many live in your garden or local park and how their behaviour and numbers change over a month.

1. Pick an organism you wish to study. Don't pick anything you won't be able to find easily. For example, there's no point choosing lions (unless you live in a safari park of course)!
2. Devise a way to work out the population of the animal.
3. Monitor the population over a month (choose how many times you would like to check the population) and record and explain any changes you notice.

Use the ACE Learning Ladder to help you do your best.

Use your own words throughout the project.

Use the Good Project Guide sheet for tips on internet safety, research and literacy.

RESEARCH TIPS
When you research, follow these tips:
- How will you choose the creature you will monitor?
- How will you recognise and identify it?
- How will you calculate the population? Remember you won't be able to count every single organism.
- How will you record your data?
- How often will you need to record the creature's numbers to be able to look for patterns?

Living creatures are all around us. You may think there isn't any wildlife in your back garden, but there are probably hundreds of creatures right under your nose!

You are going to choose a living creature to investigate and try to find out how many live in your garden or local park and how their behaviour and numbers change over a month.

1. Pick an organism you wish to study. Don't pick anything you won't be able to find easily. For example, there's no point choosing lions (unless you live in a safari park of course)!
2. Devise a way to work out the population of the animal.
3. Monitor the population over a month (choose how many times you would like to check the population) and record and explain any changes you notice.

Use the ACE Learning Ladder to help you do your best.

Use your own words throughout the project.

Use the Good Project Guide sheet for tips on internet safety, research and literacy.

RESEARCH TIPS
When you research, follow these tips:
- How will you choose the creature you will monitor?
- How will you recognise and identify it?
- How will you calculate the population? Remember you won't be able to count every single organism.
- How will you record your data?
- How often will you need to record the creature's numbers to be able to look for patterns?

BIOLOGY HOMEWORK TASKS: TASK SHEET (ADVANCED)

ACE LEARNING LADDER

Assessment Check	The types of things you can do:
Advanced	• Carry out a detailed investigation, drawing on detailed scientific knowledge and understanding. • Use a preliminary study or secondary sources to design a method that will ensure creatures are counted only once each time. • Explain how repeats would be needed, and at what interval, to ensure reliability of results. • Use results to calculate a population for your creature, suggesting margins of error in these results. • Suggest and justify improvements to your method. • Use a range of scientific words, symbols and units accurately.
Confident	• Carry out an investigation, drawing on scientific knowledge and understanding. • Explain how to count creatures in as accurate a way as possible, identifying any equipment needed, so that creatures do not get recounted. • Explain how many times the creatures would need to be counted and at what interval. • Record your data in an appropriate table or graph. • Describe the pattern shown in your results, concluding by giving an approximate population for your creature and evaluating how reliable your results are in terms of the method you used. • Use a range of appropriate scientific words, symbols and units.
Establishing	• Carry out a basic investigation, drawing on some scientific knowledge and understanding. • State a simple method for counting the creature you have chosen. • State why it is important to carry out at least one repeat. • Record your data in a simple table and, with some help, give an estimated population for your creature. • State one way the method could be improved. • Use some appropriate scientific words, symbols and units.

NATIONAL CURRICULUM LINKS

The topic covered will depend on the focus of the investigation.

WORKING SCIENTIFICALLY
Scientific attitudes
Experimental skills and investigations
Analysis and evaluation
Measurement

CROSS-CURRICULAR OPPORTUNITIES:
- Many cross curricular links are possible, depending on the focus chosen for the investigation.

TIME

Three homework sessions of between 30 and 60 minutes each, depending on ability.

ADDITIONAL GUIDANCE

This task is completely open ended and will allow students to carry out an investigation into almost anything they would like to find out about. The task is linked with Mini Investigation 6 (My Peer Review), as it is intended to allow students to experience first-hand how the scientific method works in practice, where scientists publish their results and these are peer reviewed by other scientists. Students will need to plan, carry out and analyse an entire investigation of their choosing. They will need to write this up in full.

If you choose to use the My Peer Review task, each student will then exchange their investigation with another student who will carry out the same investigation and then compare their own findings, hence conducting a small-scale peer review. This task, along with My Peer Review, would be suitable for school science fairs or competitions. To support students, it would be beneficial to have some ideas of simple investigations they could carry out. These should be able to be carried out in a home environment; for example, they could try to determine which biscuit is the most dunkable, which felt tip pens last the longest, or which sweets are the chewiest.

Student plans will need to be checked for safety aspects before the practical work is carried out, and it is up to you to ensure this happens.

ASSESSMENT, FEEDBACK AND IMPROVEMENT

Assessing these tasks should not be arduous. Rather than assigning an absolute grade, you should focus on how each student can improve. To ensure that this task is formative, students should be given the opportunity to improve their work based on the teacher's targets or through peer and self-assessment.

GUIDANCE FOR CONFIDENT (C)

Students working with confidence choose a fair, reliable method and make conclusions based on their results.

We find that reading through the project using these additional prompts helps to assess the task.

Scientists through the centuries have investigated things that interested them, from the ancient Greeks wondering about what everything was made from to scientists today trying to find out if there is life on other planets.

Now it is your turn to investigate something that interests you. Your teacher may suggest some investigations for you to choose from, or you can choose something to find out about yourself. The only rule is, you must investigate it scientifically!

You will need to write up your investigation in full so that another student could read it and know exactly what you were investigating, how you carried it out and what you found out.

Your investigation should have the following parts:

PLANNING
- What are you trying to find out?
- What method will you use?
  How will you make it fair and scientific?
- How will you stay safe?

CARRYING OUT
- How did you obtain results/make observations?
- How did you record them?
- How did you make sure you didn't make mistakes?

ANALYSING YOUR RESULTS
- Which is the best way to display your results (e.g. a graph or table)?
- Are there any patterns in your results? How did you spot these?
- Can you reach an overall conclusion from your investigation that answers the question you first had?

EVALUATING
- What was good about your investigation – how did this affect your results?
- What was bad about your investigation – how did this affect your results?
- How would you improve your investigation if you did it again?
- Do you think you can trust what you have found out? Why?

Use the ACE Learning Ladder to help you do your best.

Use your own words throughout the project.

Use the Good Project Guide sheet for tips on internet safety, research and literacy.

MY SCIENTIFIC INVESTIGATION

Scientists through the centuries have investigated things that interested them, from the ancient Greeks wondering about what everything was made from to scientists today trying to find out if there is life on other planets.

Now it is your turn to investigate something that interests you. Your teacher may suggest some investigations for you to choose from, or you can choose something to find out about yourself. The only rule is, you must investigate it scientifically!

You will need to write up your investigation in full so that another student could read it and know exactly what you were investigating, how you carried it out and what you found out.

Your investigation should have the following parts:

PLANNING
- What method will you use and why?
- How will you stay safe?

CARRYING OUT
- How did you obtain results, making sure they were as accurate and precise as possible?
- How have you recorded your results?

ANALYSING YOUR RESULTS
- Your results should be displayed in an appropriate format.
- What patterns are in your results?
- What is your overall conclusion?

EVALUATING
- Do you think anything about your investigation could have been better? Why?
- Do you think you can trust what you have found out? Why?

Use the ACE Learning Ladder to help you do your best.

Use your own words throughout the project.

Use the Good Project Guide sheet for tips on internet safety, research and literacy.

Scientists through the centuries have investigated things that interested them, from the ancient Greeks wondering about what everything was made from to scientists today trying to find out if there is life on other planets.

Now it is your turn to investigate something that interests you. Your teacher may suggest some investigations for you to choose from, or you can choose something to find out about yourself. The only rule is, you must investigate it scientifically!

You will need to write up your investigation in full so that another student could read it and know exactly what you were investigating, how you carried it out and what you found out.

Your investigation should have the following parts:
• Planning
• Carrying out
• Analysing your results
• Evaluating.

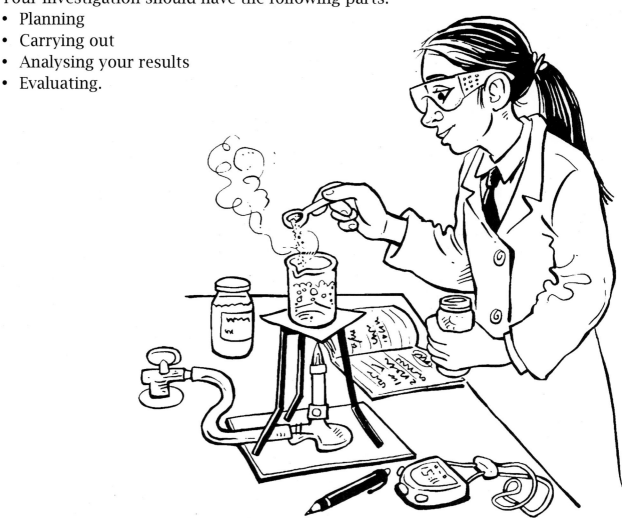

Use the ACE Learning Ladder to help you do your best.

Use your own words throughout the project.

Use the Good Project Guide sheet for tips on internet safety, research and literacy.

ACE LEARNING LADDER

Assessment Check	The types of things you can do:
Advanced	• Carry out a detailed investigation, drawing on detailed scientific knowledge and understanding. • Use preliminary research to plan a detailed method which allows you to answer the question you have chosen and shows how you will be accurate and precise. • Obtain results that show a suitable number of repeats, identifying anomalies. • Use a detailed graph or table to display your results and describe, in detail, any patterns observed. • Give a detailed conclusion, explaining how your results justify this. • Suggest and explain improvements and whether your results are reliable, explaining why anomalies may have arisen. • Use a range of scientific words, symbols and units accurately.
Confident	• Carry out an investigation, drawing on scientific knowledge and understanding. • Plan a method which allows you to answer your question and shows how you will be accurate and precise. • Obtain results that show a suitable number of repeats. • Use a graph or table to display your results and describe any patterns observed. • State a conclusion, explaining how your results justify this. • Suggest and explain improvements and whether your results are reliable. • Use a range of appropriate scientific words, symbols and units.
Establishing	• Carry out a simple investigation, drawing on some scientific knowledge and understanding. • Plan a simple method to answer your question. • Obtain results, using some repeats. • Use a graph or table to display your results and describe any overall pattern your results show. • State a simple conclusion. • Suggest one improvement to your investigation. • Use some appropriate scientific words, symbols and units.

NATIONAL CURRICULUM LINKS

The topic covered will depend on the focus of the investigation.

WORKING SCIENTIFICALLY
Scientific attitudes
Experimental skills and investigations
Analysis and evaluation
Measurement

CROSS–CURRICULAR OPPORTUNITIES:
- Many cross-curricular links are possible, depending on the focus chosen for the investigation.

TIME

Three homework sessions of between 30 and 60 minutes each, depending on ability.

ADDITIONAL GUIDANCE

This can be a stand-alone task, for students to peer review an investigation of your choice; however, ideally it should follow the My Scientific Investigation task (Mini Investigation 2). Students will need to be given a copy of another student's full investigation (or an investigation of your choice if you are not using the task as a follow-up to Mini Investigation 2). The students will need to follow the method provided, and gather their own set of results in order to compare the conclusion they draw with the conclusion drawn by their fellow student. This task will allow students to consider how peer review works and the purpose of peer review. Students should be familiar with the concept of peer review before this task and would also benefit from having seen some examples of journals containing research findings.

It is your responsibility to ensure that the investigations handed out for this task are safe, and suitable for use in a home environment.

ASSESSMENT, FEEDBACK AND IMPROVEMENT

Assessing these tasks should not be arduous. Rather than assigning an absolute grade, you should focus on how each student can improve. To ensure that this task is formative, students should be given the opportunity to improve their work based on the teacher's targets or through peer and self-assessment.

GUIDANCE FOR CONFIDENT (C)

Students working with confidence make conclusions based on their results.

We find that reading through the project using these additional prompts helps to assess the task.

Scientists carry out investigations and publish their results for other scientists to see. Other scientists will check if they agree with the results and findings, and may try the investigation themselves to see if they get the same results.

When scientists check and review each other's work in this way it is known as **peer review**. Peer review is a vital part of scientific research and helps ensure that scientific findings are tested and reliable.

Your teacher will provide you with an investigation, possibly from one of your classmates, that will include a method, results and a conclusion. You are going to peer review this investigation by carrying it out yourself to obtain your own results. You will use your set of results to decide if you are confident that the conclusion in the original investigation was correct.

When you carry out your peer review you need to write a report that covers the following points:
- What was the investigation trying to find out?
- Was the method suitable to answer this question?
- What results have you obtained? How will you record these?
- Did you follow the method exactly?
- How have you made sure you didn't make any mistakes?
- Are there any patterns in your results?
- Are the patterns in the results the same as those in the original results?
- Can you give an overall conclusion from your results to answer the original question?
- Is your conclusion the same as the original conclusion? Why?
- How do you know your set of results can be trusted?

Use the ACE Learning Ladder to help you do your best.

Use your own words throughout the project.

Use the Good Project Guide sheet for tips on internet safety, research and literacy.

BIOLOGY HOMEWORK TASKS: TASK SHEET (ESTABLISHING)

Scientists carry out investigations and publish their results for other scientists to see. Other scientists will check if they agree with the results and findings, and may try the investigation themselves to see if they get the same results.

When scientists check and review each other's work in this way it is known as **peer review**. Peer review is a vital part of scientific research and helps ensure that scientific findings are tested and reliable.

Your teacher will provide you with an investigation, possibly from one of your classmates, that will include a method, results and a conclusion. You are going to peer review this investigation by carrying it out yourself to obtain your own results. You will use your set of results to decide if you are confident that the conclusion in the original investigation was correct.

When you carry out your peer review you need to write a report that covers the following points:
- What was the investigation trying to find out?
- Was the method suitable to answer this question?
- How have you made sure you didn't make any mistakes?
- Are the patterns in your results the same as those in the original results?
- Is your conclusion the same as the original conclusion? Why?
- How do you know your set of results can be trusted?

Use websites, magazines and books to get information. Use the ACE Learning Ladder to help you do your best.

Use your own words throughout the project.

Use the Good Project Guide sheet for tips on internet safety, research and literacy.

Scientists carry out investigations and publish their results for other scientists to see. Other scientists will check if they agree with the results and findings, and may try the investigation themselves to see if they get the same results.

When scientists check and review each other's work in this way it is known as **peer review**. Peer review is a vital part of scientific research and helps ensure that scientific findings are tested and reliable.

Your teacher will provide you with an investigation, possibly from one of your classmates, that will include a method, results and a conclusion. You are going to peer review this investigation by carrying it out yourself to obtain your own results. You will use your set of results to decide if you are confident that the conclusion in the original investigation was correct.

When you carry out your peer review you need to write a report that covers the following points:
- Was the method suitable for answering the original question posed? Why?
- How did you ensure differences that occurred were not due to you?
- Are the patterns in the results the same as in the original results?
- Is your conclusion the same as the original conclusion?
- How do you know your set of results can be trusted?

Use websites, magazines and books to get information. Use the ACE Learning Ladder to help you do your best.

Use your own words throughout the project.

Use the Good Project Guide sheet for tips on internet safety, research and literacy.

ACE LEARNING LADDER

Assessment Check	The types of things you can do:
Advanced	• Carry out a detailed peer review. • Explain whether the method was suitable to answer the question and how the integrity of results was ensured. • Obtain results that show a suitable number of repeats, with any anomalies identified. • Use a detailed graph or table to display your results and describe, again in detail, any patterns observed. • Give a detailed and justified conclusion, comparing this with the original conclusion, and suggesting reasons for any differences. • Explain, giving a degree of uncertainty, why your own set of results are adequate enough to confirm or challenge the original conclusion. • Use a range of scientific words, symbols and units accurately.
Confident	• Carry out a peer review. • Explain whether the method was suitable for answering the question being investigated. • Obtain results that show a suitable number of repeats. • Use graphs or tables to display your results and describe patterns observed. • Give a conclusion, explaining how your results justify this and comparing this with the original conclusion. • Explain why your own set of results are adequate enough to confirm or challenge the original conclusion. • Use a range of appropriate scientific words, symbols and units.
Establishing	• Carry out a simple peer review. • State how you would make sure you did not make mistakes when following the original method. • Obtain results with some repeats. • Use a graph or table to display your results and describe any overall pattern your results show. • Give a conclusion, and describe whether this is the same or different to the original conclusion. • State your opinion on whether the original conclusion was correct or not and why you think this. • Use some appropriate scientific words, symbols and units.

MINI INVESTIGATION 4: TEACHER NOTES
PERCEPTIONS OF SCIENCE

NATIONAL CURRICULUM LINKS

Any topics covered will depend on the focus of the investigation.

WORKING SCIENTIFICALLY
Scientific attitudes
Experimental skills and investigations
Analysis and evaluation
Measurement

CROSS–CURRICULAR OPPORTUNITIES INCLUDE:
- mathematics – interpretation of results; design of survey.

TIME

Three homework sessions of between 30 and 60 minutes each, depending on ability.

ADDITIONAL GUIDANCE

This is a very open-ended task, for which students will need no prior background knowledge. Students should be given as much freedom as possible to develop their own questions for the survey. For lower ability students you may like to come up with a pool of questions for students to choose from and then focus more on the analysis of results when marking the task.

ASSESSMENT, FEEDBACK AND IMPROVEMENT

Assessing these tasks should not be arduous. Rather than assigning an absolute grade, you should focus on how each student can improve. To ensure that this task is formative, students should be given the opportunity to improve their work based on the teacher's targets or through peer and self-assessment.

GUIDANCE FOR CONFIDENT (C)

Students working with confidence choose a fair, reliable method and make conclusions based on their results.

We find that reading through the project using these additional prompts helps to assess the task.

What do you think people really think about science? Is it seen as really exciting or really boring? Do people assume all scientists are men, or wear white coats? Or is it seen as too hard to understand?

- Design a survey to find out what people really think about science.
- Decide how many people will need to complete your survey to make the results reflect what people really think (i.e. don't just ask one person!).
- Look through all the results and prepare a report on what you have found out.
- Try and give reasons for the perceptions people have about science.

It is up to you to decide how to carry out this investigation. You will need to produce a written plan and record your results. Present your results and draw a conclusion, then evaluate your investigation.

Use websites, magazines and books to get information. Use the ACE Learning Ladder to help you do your best.

Use your own words throughout the investigation.

Use the Good Project Guide sheet for tips on internet safety, research and literacy.

INVESTIGATION TIPS

Planning
- Think about the question you are answering.

Considering
- Decide how to present your results.
- Describe and explain the pattern in your results.

Evaluating
- Consider how your investigation could be improved.

PERCEPTIONS OF SCIENCE

What do you think people really think about science? Is it seen as really exciting or really boring? Do people assume all scientists are men, or wear white coats? Or is it seen as too hard to understand?

- Design a survey to find out what people really think about science.
- Decide how many people will need to complete your survey to make the results reflect what people really think (i.e. don't just ask one person!).
- Look through all the results and prepare a report on what you have found out and why you think this is.

It is up to you to decide how to carry out this investigation. You will need to produce a written plan and record your results. Present your results and draw a conclusion, then evaluate your investigation.

Use websites, magazines and books to get information. Use the ACE Learning Ladder to help you do your best.

Use your own words throughout the investigation.

Use the Good Project Guide sheet for tips on internet safety, research and literacy.

INVESTIGATION TIPS

Planning
- Think about the question you are answering.
- Do a preliminary study to inform your plan.
- How can you make your survey reliable?

Obtaining
- Design a table to include all your results.
- Decide how to present your results.

Considering
- Describe and explain the pattern in your results.

Evaluating
- What are the strengths and weaknesses of your investigation?
- Consider how it could be improved.

What do you think people really think about science? Is it seen as really exciting or really boring? Do people assume all scientists are men, or wear white coats? Or is it seen as too hard to understand?

- Design a survey to find out what people really think about science.
- The results of your survey should give a good representation of what people think about science and why they think those things.

It is up to you to decide how to carry out this investigation. You will need to produce a written plan and record your results. Present your results and draw a conclusion, then evaluate your investigation.

Use websites, magazines and books to get information. Use the ACE Learning Ladder to help you do your best.

Use your own words throughout the investigation.

Use the Good Project Guide sheet for tips on internet safety, research and literacy.

INVESTIGATION TIPS

When you investigate, consider these points:

Planning
- What are the main parts of a plan?
- How will you collect and record your results?
- How will you present your results?

Considering
- How will you describe and explain your results?

Evaluating
- What are the strengths and weaknesses of your investigation?
- Consider how it could be improved.

ACE LEARNING LADDER

Assessment Check	The types of things you can do:
Advanced	• Carry out a detailed investigation, drawing on detailed scientific knowledge and understanding. • Use secondary resources to help plan an accurate and reliable investigation. Formulate suitable questions and justify your sample size. • Present your results suitably and accurately. • Analyse your results to show any patterns and compare these with previously published figures on perceptions of science. • Justify the conclusion you reach from your investigation. • Evaluate your investigation, suggesting how any drawbacks could be overcome in subsequent investigations. • Use a range of scientific words, symbols and units accurately.
Confident	• Carry out an investigation, drawing on scientific knowledge and understanding. • Decide on suitable questions and sample size. • Explain how your investigation will produce valid, accurate and reliable results. • Present your results in an appropriate table or graph and identify any patterns within them. • Draw a conclusion from your investigation, using evidence from your results to justify this. • Suggest a strength and weakness of your investigation. • Use a range of appropriate scientific words, symbols and units.
Establishing	• Carry out a simple investigation, drawing on some scientific knowledge and understanding. • Identify how many people you will need to question and the questions you will use. • Survey at least three people, recording their answers in a suitable table. • With help, draw a simple graph of your results. • State what your results show. • List one way to improve your investigation. • Use some appropriate scientific words, symbols and units.

3 MINI INVESTIGATION 5: TEACHER NOTES
SCREEN SCIENTISTS

NATIONAL CURRICULUM LINKS

WORKING SCIENTIFICALLY
Scientific attitudes
Experimental skills and investigations
Analysis and evaluation
Measurement

CROSS-CURRICULAR OPPORTUNITIES INCLUDE:

- English – examining various forms of media, writing up findings
- citizenship – considering stereotypes
- ICT – internet searches, evaluating websites, word processing.

TIME

Three homework sessions of between 30 and 60 minutes each, depending on ability.

ADDITIONAL GUIDANCE

Students need very little scientific knowledge to complete this task but should be familiar with the stages that need to be followed when undertaking a scientific investigation. Students could be asked to come up with their idea of what everyday scientists look like and behave like. A range of sources showing scientists could then be examined together before the task is explained. Emphasis should be placed on keeping the investigation fair and balanced, even though the investigation may seem very different to typical practical investigations.

ASSESSMENT, FEEDBACK AND IMPROVEMENT

Assessing these tasks should not be arduous. Rather than assigning an absolute grade, you should focus on how each student can improve. To ensure that this task is formative, students should be given the opportunity to improve their work based on the teacher's targets or through peer and self-assessment.

GUIDANCE FOR CONFIDENT (C)

Students working with confidence choose a fair, reliable method and make conclusions based on their results.

We find that reading through the project using these additional prompts helps to assess the task.

Have you ever heard scientists, or people who like science, being described as geeks or nerds? When someone says 'scientist' do you think of a crazy looking man wearing a white coat and with strange hair?

Do you think this stereotypeical image of scientists is fair or true? Perhaps the image is just based on a few scientists or it's been exaggerated to make films entertaining. Use secondary sources (e.g. films, newspapers, magazines) to investigate how scientists are portrayed.

1. Find your secondary sources and look for pictures or descriptions of scientists from TV and films.
2. Investigate how many of these sources portray scientists in the ways mentioned above. Use what you find out to come up with your own ideas about what a typical scientist is like.
3. Display what you find out in a poster that could be used for a class discussion.

TIPS

1. Make sure you find lots of pictures of scientists, from lots of different places.

2. Does the image of the scientist fit the stereotype described above?

3. Draw a table to show what you find out from each image or description you choose.

4. Find some examples of what real life scientists are like. Do they differ from the stereotype?

5. What do you think about scientists after your investigation?

Use websites, magazines and books to get information. Use the ACE Learning Ladder to help you do your best.

Use your own words throughout the project.

Use the Good Project Guide sheet for tips on internet safety, research and literacy.

Have you ever heard scientists, or people who like science, being described as geeks or nerds? When someone says 'scientist' do you think of a crazy looking man wearing a white coat and with strange hair?

Do you think this stereotypeical image of scientists is fair or true? Perhaps the image is just based on a few scientists or it's been exaggerated to make films entertaining. Use secondary sources (e.g. films, newspapers, magazines) to investigate how scientists are portrayed.

1. Find your secondary sources and look for pictures or descriptions of scientists.
2. Investigate how many of these sources portray scientists in the ways mentioned above. Design a poster that compares how scientists are portrayed in films and TV to scientists in real life.
3. Display what you find out in a poster that presents your argument.

TIPS

1. Choose several pictures or descriptions of scientists from different sources.

2. Does the image of the scientist fit the stereotype?

3. You could record information about your different sources in a table.

4. Find some examples of what real-life scientists are like. Do they differ from the stereotype?

5. What do you think about scientists after your investigation?

Use websites, magazines and books to get information. Use the ACE Learning Ladder to help you do your best.

Use your own words throughout the project.

Use the Good Project Guide sheet for tips on internet safety, research and literacy.

Have you ever heard scientists, or people who like science, being described as geeks or nerds? When someone says 'scientist' do you think of a crazy looking man wearing a white coat and with strange hair?

Do you think this stereotypeical image of scientists is fair or true? Perhaps the image is just based on a few scientists or it's been exaggerated to make films entertaining. Use secondary sources (e.g. films, newspapers, magazines) to investigate how scientists are portrayed.

1. Find your secondary sources and look for pictures or descriptions of scientists in films and those in real life.
2. Investigate how many of these sources portray scientists in the ways mentioned above. Design a poster that compares how scientists are portrayed in films and TV to scientists in real life.
3. Ensure your poster presents your argument.

Points to consider:
1. How many images or descriptions will you need to review?
2. How will you judge whether they fit the stereotype?
3. How will you record the information you find out?
4. Can you find some examples of what real-life scientists are like — do they differ from the stereotype?
5. What do you think about scientists after your investigation?

Use websites, magazines and books to get information. Use the ACE Learning Ladder to help you do your best.

Use your own words throughout the project.

Use the Good Project Guide sheet for tips on internet safety, research and literacy.

ACE LEARNING LADDER

Assessment Check	The types of things you can do:
Advanced	• Carry out a detailed investigation into scientific image, drawing on detailed scientific knowledge and understanding. • Explain how you ensured your selection of secondary sources ensured a fair representation of images of scientists in general. • Where possible, describe your results quantitatively, and identify patterns within your results (e.g. differences according to the types of source). • Present your results appropriately. • Give a conclusion from your results, using evidence from your findings to back this up, but also identifying weaknesses in your results. • Suggest next steps for the investigation. • Use a range of scientific words, symbols and units accurately.
Confident	• Carry out an investigation into images of scientists, drawing on scientific knowledge and understanding. • Identify how to collect your data on images, justifying why this is a fair method. • Decide on a suitable number of sources to review, justifying your choice. • Choose suitable ways to present your findings, e.g. a graph or table. • Give a conclusion from your results, using evidence from your findings to back this up. • Use a range of appropriate scientific words, symbols and units.
Establishing	• Carry out a simple investigation into images of scientists, drawing on some scientific knowledge and understanding. • Select secondary sources from at least four different places. • Describe the image shown in each secondary source used. • Use a table or simple graph to present your results. • State a simple conclusion about whether the secondary sources fitted the stereotype. • Use some appropriate scientific words, symbols and units.

4

CRITICAL THINKING 1: TEACHER NOTES
STEM CELLS – YES OR NO?

NATIONAL CURRICULUM LINKS

CELLS AND ORGANISATION
- cells as the fundamental unit of living organisms, including how to observe, interpret and record cell structure using a light microscope
- the functions of the cell wall, cell membrane, cytoplasm, nucleus, vacuole, mitochondria and chloroplasts
- the hierarchical organisation of multicellular organisms: from cells to tissues to organs to systems to organisms.

WORKING SCIENTIFICALLY
Scientific attitudes
Analysis and evaluation

CROSS–CURRICULAR OPPORTUNITIES INCLUDE:
- citizenship – ethical issues.

TIME

Two homework sessions of between 30 and 60 minutes each, depending on ability.

ADDITIONAL GUIDANCE

This can be used as a stand-alone task. However, it would fit well with any topic covering health and disease, perhaps cells/tissues and organs, or ethical and moral issues.

It may be advisable to provide selected information to students of lower ability to ensure that they do not use websites which are unsuitable due to their scientific language or are too in depth for what is required for the task. Students need to find information about what stem cells are and whether they feel their use is something they agree with or not, or if they are suitable only for some circumstances.

ASSESSMENT, FEEDBACK AND IMPROVEMENT

Assessing these tasks should not be arduous. Rather than assigning an absolute grade, you should focus on how each student can improve. To ensure that this task is formative, students should be given the opportunity to improve their work based on the teacher's targets or through peer and self-assessment.

GUIDANCE FOR CONFIDENT (C)

Students working with confidence can present two perspectives and justify their own viewpoint.

We find that reading through the project using these additional prompts helps to assess the task.

STEM CELLS – YES OR NO?

Have you ever heard of stem cells? Some scientists believe they hold the key to curing many people of illness and disease. However, other people don't agree with their use or are concerned about where the use of stem cells may lead.

Write a letter to your MP about whether you think stems cells should be used in medical research.

You should:
- research what a stem cell is
- include information about why stem cells may be useful in the treatment of certain illnesses or diseases
- find out why some people are not in favour of the use of stem cells
- decide whether you think stem cells should be used, giving some information about how you decided.

Use the ACE Learning Ladder to help you do your best.

Use your own words throughout the project.

Use the Good Project Guide sheet for tips on internet safety, research and literacy.

STEM CELLS – YES OR NO?

Have you ever heard of stem cells? Some scientists believe they hold the key to curing many people of illness and disease. However, other people don't agree with their use or are concerned about where the use of stem cells may lead.

Write a letter to your MP about whether you think stems cells should be used in medical research.

You should:
- research what a stem cell is and how they work within the human body
- include information about how stem cells may be useful in the treatment of certain illnesses or disease
- research the different opinions people have on the use of stem cells
- decide whether you think stem cells should be used, giving some information about how you decided.

Use the ACE Learning Ladder to help you do your best.

Use your own words throughout the project.

Use the Good Project Guide sheet for tips on internet safety, research and literacy.

CRITICAL THINKING 1: TASK SHEET (ADVANCED)
STEM CELLS – YES OR NO?

Have you ever heard of stem cells? Some scientists believe they hold the key to curing many people of illness and disease. However, other people don't agree with their use or are concerned about where the use of stem cells may lead.

Write a letter to your MP about whether you think stems cells should be used in medical research.

You should decide how to set out your letter and what information to include in it.

Use the ACE Learning Ladder to help you do your best.

Use your own words throughout the project.

Use the Good Project Guide sheet for tips on internet safety, research and literacy.

BIOLOGY HOMEWORK TASKS: TASK SHEET (ADVANCED)

4

ACE LEARNING LADDER

Assessment Check	The types of things you can do:
Advanced	• Write a detailed letter, drawing on detailed scientific knowledge and understanding. • Explain what stem cells are and why they may be of great use, using cell diagrams to explain how they differ from other cells. • Explain the viewpoints of those in favour of stem cell research and those who disagree with it, classifying viewpoints as fact, opinion and speculation. • Explain how stem cell research is carried out and why this may pose moral and ethical concerns. • Give a detailed opinion on stem cell research, using several sources of evidence to justify your overall opinion. • Use a range of scientific words, symbols and units accurately.
Confident	• Write a letter, drawing on scientific knowledge and understanding. • Explain what stem cells are and why they may be of great use. • Explain the viewpoints of those in favour of stem cell research and those who disagree with stem cell research. • Explain the science involved in it. • Give your opinion on stem cell research, using evidence to justify your overall opinion. • Use a range of appropriate scientific words, symbols and units.
Establishing	• Write a simple letter, drawing on some scientific knowledge and understanding. • State what stem cells are and why scientists want to find out about them. • Describe an advantage and disadvantage of stem cell research. • State one or two viewpoints about stem cell research. • Describe some aspects of science that would be relevant to a scientist researching stem cells. • Use some appropriate scientific words, symbols and units.

CRITICAL THINKING 2: TEACHER NOTES
TISSUE ISSUES

NATIONAL CURRICULUM LINKS

CELLS AND ORGANISATION
- the hierarchical organisation of multicellular organisms: from cells to tissues to organs to systems to organisms.

WORKING SCIENTIFICALLY
Experimental skills and investigations
Analysis and evaluation
Measurement

CROSS–CURRICULAR OPPORTUNITIES INCLUDE:
- English – writing a summary
- ICT – internet searching, word processing
- citizenship – our individual role in society.

TIME

Two homework sessions of between 30 and 60 minutes each, depending on ability.

ADDITIONAL GUIDANCE

Check for students who may be sensitive about the issue of organ donation before setting the task. You may need to find and suggest suitable websites for students who are Establishing.

ASSESSMENT, FEEDBACK AND IMPROVEMENT

Assessing these tasks should not be arduous. Rather than assigning an absolute grade, you should focus on how each student can improve. To ensure that this task is formative, students should be given the opportunity to improve their work based on the teacher's targets or through peer and self-assessment.

GUIDANCE FOR CONFIDENT (C)

Students working with confidence can present evidence and justifications.

We find that reading through the project using these additional prompts helps to assess the task.

Sometimes people suffer with severe diseases of major organs such as the heart, lungs or kidneys. Doctors can sometimes help patients by performing transplants of these organs from people who have recently died. This is called organ donation.

In some countries there is an 'opt-in' scheme, where people carry donor cards if they want to donate their organs when they die. In other countries there is an 'opt-out' scheme, where people have to register if they do not want their organs used for transplants.

Find out about organ donation and the issues about it. Try to find out about:
• how an 'opt-in' scheme works
• how an 'opt-out' scheme works
• which countries have each type of scheme
• the advantages and disadvantages of organ donation
• people's feelings about organ donation.

Decide which system you think is best: the 'opt in' (carry a donor card if you wish to donate your organs) or 'opt out' (everyone donates unless they say they do not wish to).

Write a letter to your MP; tell them which organ donation scheme you think is best and why you have made this decision.

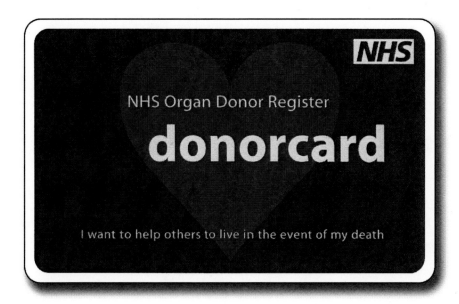

Use the ACE Learning Ladder to help you do your best.

Use your own words throughout the project.

Use the Good Project Guide sheet for tips on internet safety, research and literacy.

Sometimes people suffer with severe diseases of major organs such as the heart, lungs or kidneys. Doctors can help patients by performing transplants of these organs from people who have recently died. This is called organ donation.

In some countries there is an 'opt-in' scheme, where people carry donor cards if they want to donate their organs when they die. In other countries there is an 'opt-out' scheme, where people have to register if they do not want their organs used for transplants.

Research the issues about organ donation.

Decide which system you think is best: the 'opt-in' (carry a donor card if you wish to donate your organs) or 'opt-out' (everyone donates unless they say they do not wish to).

Write a letter to your MP, setting out your argument.

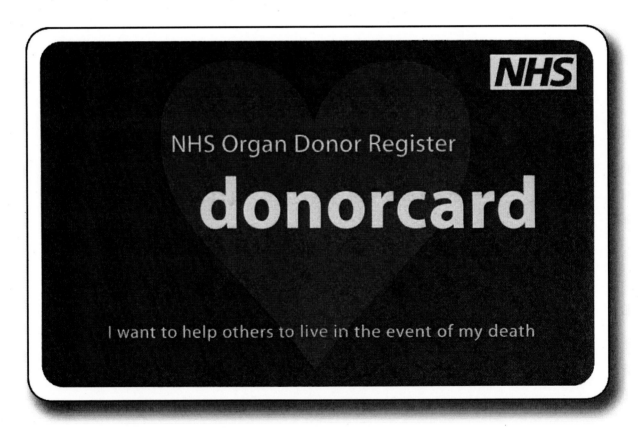

Use the ACE Learning Ladder to help you do your best.

Use your own words throughout the project.

Use the Good Project Guide sheet for tips on internet safety, research and literacy.

Sometimes people suffer with severe diseases of major organs such as the heart, lungs or kidneys. Doctors can help patients by performing transplants of these organs from people who have recently died. This is called organ donation.

Research the issues about organ donation, including 'opt-in' and 'opt-out' schemes that let people express their views on whether they wish to donate their organs after they die.

Write a letter to your MP, setting out and explaining your opinions on organ donation and whether an opt-in scheme or an opt-out scheme should be used.

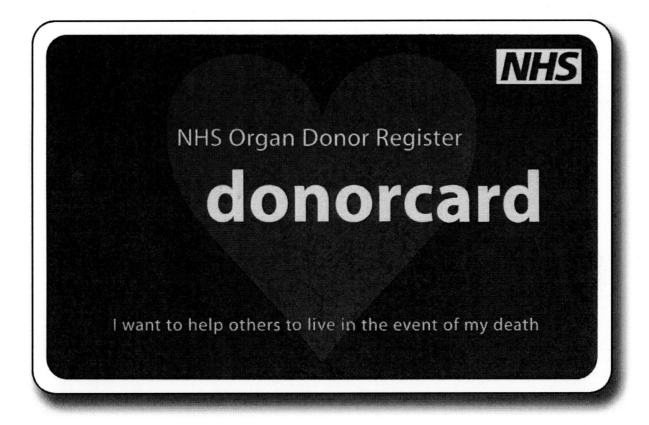

Use the ACE Learning Ladder to help you do your best.

Use your own words throughout the project.

Use the Good Project Guide sheet for tips on internet safety, research and literacy.

4 CRITICAL THINKING 2: ACE LEARNING LADDER
TISSUE ISSUES

ACE LEARNING LADDER

Assessment Check	The types of things you can do:
Advanced	• Write a detailed letter about organ donation, drawing on detailed scientific knowledge and understanding. • Provide an in-depth explanation of the issues surrounding organ donation and opt-in and opt-out schemes. • Make several points, each supported by evidence. • Offer your opinion on which scheme is best, quoting several pieces of evidence to justify your conclusion. • Suggest further information that is needed to make informed choices about the various organ donation schemes. • Use a range of scientific words, symbols and units accurately.
Confident	• Write a letter about organ donation, drawing on scientific knowledge and understanding. • Explain the main issues surrounding organ donation and opt-in and opt-out schemes. • Make three points, each supported by evidence. • Offer your opinion on which scheme is best, explaining how the evidence influenced your conclusion. • Quote figures and findings from your research appropriately, e.g. using statistics or graphs. • Use a range of appropriate scientific words, symbols and units.
Establishing	• Write a simple letter about organ donation, drawing on some scientific knowledge and understanding. • State why organ donation is important and some issues involved in it. • State one or two points, including some evidence for each. • State your opinion on which scheme is best. • Use some scientific words and units when discussing organ transplants.

NATIONAL CURRICULUM LINKS

CELLS AND ORGANISATION
- cells as the fundamental unit of living organisms, including how to observe, interpret and record cell structure using a light microscope
- the functions of the cell wall, cell membrane, cytoplasm, nucleus, vacuole, mitochondria and chloroplasts.

NUTRITION AND DIGESTION
- content of a healthy human diet: carbohydrates, lipids (fats and oils), proteins, vitamins, minerals, dietary fibre and water, and why each is needed
- the consequences of imbalances in the diet, including obesity, starvation and deficiency diseases
- the tissues and organs of the human digestive system, including adaptations to function and how the digestive system digests food (enzymes simply as biological catalysts).

WORKING SCIENTIFICALLY
Experimental skills and investigations
Analysis and evaluation

CROSS-CURRICULAR OPPORTUNITIES INCLUDE:
- food technology – knowledge of vitamins and balanced diet.

TIME

Two homework sessions of between 30 and 60 minutes each, depending on ability.

ADDITIONAL GUIDANCE

Students will need some knowledge of food and nutrition before tackling this task. Students should be encouraged to research the topic using many different sources to find out whether vitamins are considered beneficial by the health/medical professions. In-depth explanation of how vitamins work or their chemical make-up is not required for this task.

ASSESSMENT, FEEDBACK AND IMPROVEMENT

Assessing these tasks should not be arduous. Rather than assigning an absolute grade, you should focus on how each student can improve. To ensure that this task is formative, students should be given the opportunity to improve their work based on the teacher's targets or through peer and self-assessment.

GUIDANCE FOR CONFIDENT (C)

Students working with confidence can use evidence to inform their report.

We find that reading through the project using these additional prompts helps to assess the task.

4 VIEWS ON VITAMINS

We are always being told about the importance of eating a balanced diet, taking enough exercise and drinking plenty of water so that we stay healthy. Many people claim that taking vitamins can help us achieve this. Is it necessary to take vitamins, though?

Find out all about vitamins and what they can do for us, then prepare a report which your local doctors' surgery could hand out to patients.

Your report should include:
• what vitamins are and how they work
• examples of what each vitamin (e.g. vitamin D) is needed for in the body
• whether health professionals agree we should take them
• whether dieticians think they are necessary
• other ways to get vitamins without having to take vitamin pills.

Use the ACE Learning Ladder to help you do your best.

Use your own words throughout the project.

Use the Good Project Guide sheet for tips on internet safety, research and literacy.

We are always being told about the importance of eating a balanced diet, taking enough exercise and drinking plenty of water so that we stay healthy. Many people claim that taking vitamins can help us achieve this. Is it necessary to take vitamins, though?

Find out all about vitamins and what they can do for us, then prepare a report which your local doctors' surgery could hand out to patients.

Your report should include:
- what vitamin tablets are
- why people need vitamins
- the views of a range of people about taking vitamin tablets
- any alternatives to taking vitamins.

Use the ACE Learning Ladder to help you do your best.

Use your own words throughout the project.

Use The Good Project Guide Sheet for tips on Internet safety, Research and Literacy.

We are always being told about the importance of eating a balanced diet, taking enough exercise and drinking plenty of water so that we stay healthy. Many people claim that taking vitamins can help us achieve this. Is it necessary to take vitamins, though?

Find out all about vitamins and what they can do for us and prepare a report which your local doctors' surgery could hand out to patients.

It is up to you to decide what to include in your report and how to set it out.

Use the ACE Learning Ladder to help you do your best.

Use your own words throughout the project.

Use the Good Project Guide sheet for tips on internet safety, research and literacy.

CRITICAL THINKING 3: ACE LEARNING LADDER
VIEWS ON VITAMINS

ACE LEARNING LADDER

Assessment Check	The types of things you can do:
Advanced	• Write a detailed report on vitamins, drawing on detailed scientific knowledge and understanding. • Explain why vitamins are needed in the body, comparing this to other substances such as minerals or glucose. • Explain the role of at least eight different vitamins, and the consequences of being deficient in these. • Discuss the viewpoints of at least two different sources on vitamins, identifying whether these are evidence or opinion. • Explain how vitamins can be obtained without the need for vitamin tablets, outlining the benefits and disadvantages of each method given. • Use a range of scientific words, symbols and units accurately.
Confident	• Write a report on vitamins, drawing on scientific knowledge and understanding. • Explain why vitamins are needed in the body. • Explain the role of at least five different vitamins. • Discuss the viewpoints of at least two different sources on vitamins. • Explain how vitamins can be obtained without the need for vitamin tablets. • Use a range of appropriate scientific words, symbols and units.
Establishing	• Write a simple report on vitamins, drawing on some scientific knowledge and understanding. • State why vitamins are needed in the body. • Give examples of two or three vitamins and what they do in the body. • Identify two statements about using vitamins from secondary sources. • State two other ways of getting vitamins. • Use some appropriate scientific words, symbols and units.

CRITICAL THINKING 4: TEACHER NOTES
BEHAVIOUR BOTHER

NATIONAL CURRICULUM LINKS

NUTRITION AND DIGESTION

- content of a healthy human diet: carbohydrates, lipids (fats and oils), proteins, vitamins, minerals, dietary fibre and water, and why each is needed
- calculations of energy requirements in a healthy daily diet
- the consequences of imbalances in the diet, including obesity, starvation and deficiency diseases
- the tissues and organs of the human digestive system, including adaptations to function and how the digestive system digests food (enzymes simply as biological catalysts).

WORKING SCIENTIFICALLY
Scientific attitudes

CROSS–CURRICULAR OPPORTUNITIES INCLUDE:

- English – writing a summary
- ICT – internet searching, word processing
- food technology – food types
- citizenship – responsible behaviour.

TIME

Two homework sessions of between 30 and 60 minutes each, depending on ability.

ASSESSMENT, FEEDBACK AND IMPROVEMENT

Assessing these tasks should not be arduous. Rather than assigning an absolute grade, you should focus on how each student can improve. To ensure that this task is formative, students should be given the opportunity to improve their work based on the teacher's targets or through peer and self-assessment.

GUIDANCE FOR CONFIDENT (C)

Students working with confidence will use familiar scientific knowledge and understanding to present viewpoints and come to a conclusion.

We find that reading through the project using these additional prompts helps to assess the task.

4

BEHAVIOUR BOTHER

Does what you eat for lunch affect your behaviour?

Many studies have been done to find out if food affects people's behaviour.

You must carry out some research to find out how your behaviour is affected by food.

From your research, decide whether you think your lunch could affect your behaviour.

Write an article for the school magazine that argues your point.

PLAN FOR AN ARGUMENT

Use this table to help you plan your article.

Write down what you want to argue.	
Point 1 e.g. "I think that…"	Evidence 1 e.g. "I think this because…"
Point 2	Evidence 2
Conclusion e.g. "Overall, I think that… I think this because…"	

Use the ACE Learning Ladder to help you do your best.

Use your own words throughout the project.

Use the Good Project Guide sheet for tips on internet safety, research and literacy.

BIOLOGY HOMEWORK TASKS: TASK SHEET (ESTABLISHING)

CRITICAL THINKING 4: TASK SHEET (CONFIDENT)
BEHAVIOUR BOTHER

Does what you eat for lunch affect your behaviour?
Many studies have been done to find out if food affects people's behaviour.
You must carry out some research to find out how your behaviour is affected by food.
From your research, decide whether you think your lunch could affect your behaviour.

Write an article for the school
magazine that argues your point.

PLAN FOR AN ARGUMENT

Write down what you want to argue.	
Point 1	Evidence 1
Point 2	Evidence 2
Conclusion	

Use the ACE Learning Ladder to help you do your best.

Use your own words throughout the project.

Use the Good Project Guide sheet for tips on internet safety, research and literacy.

Does what you eat for lunch affect your behaviour?
Many studies have been done to find out if food affects people's behaviour.
You must carry out some research to find out how your behaviour is affected by food.
From your research, decide whether you think your lunch could affect your behaviour.

Write an article for the school magazine that argues your point.

SELECTION CRITERIA
• Decide on criteria to select evidence.

ARGUMENT STRUCTURE
• Plan how you are going to set out your argument.

KEYWORDS
• Decide on keywords suitable for this task.

Use the ACE Learning Ladder to help you do your best.

Use your own words throughout the project.

Use the Good Project Guide sheet for tips on internet safety, research and literacy.

CRITICAL THINKING 4: ACE LEARNING LADDER
BEHAVIOUR BOTHER

ACE LEARNING LADDER

Assessment Check	The types of things you can do:
Advanced	• Write a detailed scientific article, drawing on detailed scientific knowledge and understanding. • Research appropriate resources and critically evaluate information and evidence from these sources, explaining limitations, misrepresentation or lack of balance. • Make various points about the impact of food, supporting each with evidence and linking each to your own scientific knowledge and understanding. • Explain in detail why you chose each piece of evidence, based on the criteria. • Explain your conclusion based on the evidence you have selected, using scientific detail, and identify what further evidence would be needed to support your conclusion. • Use a range of scientific words, symbols and units accurately.
Confident	• Write a magazine article, drawing on scientific knowledge and understanding. • Research the impact of food, using books and websites, and pay attention to the reliability of the source. • Present three points about the impact of food, using evidence to support each point. • Explain how you chose each piece of evidence. • Give an overall conclusion, explaining this in terms of the evidence you have found. • Use a range of appropriate scientific words, symbols and units.
Establishing	• Write a simple article, drawing on some scientific knowledge and understanding. • Carry out research using one or two sources. • Make one or two points, giving evidence for each point. • State a conclusion about the impact of diet on behaviour. • Use some appropriate scientific words, symbols and units.

4

NATIONAL CURRICULUM LINKS

INHERITANCE, CHROMOSOMES, DNA AND GENES
- heredity as the process by which genetic information is transmitted from one generation to the next
- differences between species
- the variation between species and between individuals of the same species meaning some organisms compete more successfully, which can drive natural selection
- changes in the environment may leave individuals within a species, and some entire species, less well adapted to compete successfully and reproduce, which in turn may lead to extinction
- the importance of maintaining biodiversity and the use of gene banks to preserve hereditary material.

WORKING SCIENTIFICALLY
Analysis and evaluation

CROSS-CURRICULAR OPPORTUNITIES INCLUDE:
- citizenship – ethical issues, animal welfare.

TIME

Two homework sessions of between 30 and 60 minutes each, depending on ability.

ASSESSMENT, FEEDBACK AND IMPROVEMENT

Assessing these tasks should not be arduous. Rather than assigning an absolute grade, you should focus on how each student can improve. To ensure that this task is formative, students should be given the opportunity to improve their work based on the teacher's targets or through peer and self-assessment.

GUIDANCE FOR CONFIDENT (C)

Students working with confidence can present two perspectives and justify their own viewpoint.

We find that reading through the project using these additional prompts helps to assess the task.

CRITICAL THINKING 5: TASK SHEET (ESTABLISHING)
ARE ZOOS FOR KEEPERS?

Have you ever wondered whether a zoo is a suitable place to keep wild animals?

Do you like going to the zoo? Are they good places to help conservation of rare animals?

What are your views on keeping animals in zoos?

Research zoos and produce a background report for your school debating team. Make sure you consider the following:
• Why animals are kept in zoos.
• The advantages and disadvantages of keeping animals in zoos.
• Different people's views on keeping animals in zoos, e.g. animal rights campaigners, conservationists, zoo owners.
• Your opinion, with reasons.

Use the ACE Learning Ladder to help you do your best.

Use your own words throughout the project.

Use the Good Project Guide sheet for tips on internet safety, research and literacy.

Have you ever wondered whether a zoo is a suitable place to keep wild animals?

Do you like going to the zoo? Are they good places to help conservation of rare animals?

What are your views on keeping animals in zoos?

Research zoos and produce a background report for your school debating team. Make sure you consider the following:
- Why animals are kept in zoos.
- The advantages and disadvantages of keeping animals in zoos.
- Different people's views on keeping animals in zoos.
- The ethical, moral and economic views about keeping animals in zoos.
- The scientific knowledge that is used when keeping animals in zoos.
- Your opinion, with scientific reasons.

Use the ACE Learning Ladder to help you do your best.

Use your own words throughout the project.

Use the Good Project Guide sheet for tips on internet safety, research and literacy.

BIOLOGY HOMEWORK TASKS: TASK SHEET (CONFIDENT)

4 ARE ZOOS FOR KEEPERS?

Have you ever wondered whether a zoo is a suitable place to keep wild animals?

Do you like going to the zoo? Are they good places to help conservation of rare animals?

What are your views on keeping animals in zoos?

Research zoos and produce a background report for your school debating team. Make sure you consider the following:
• Reasons for keeping animals in zoos.
• Arguments for and against keeping animals in zoos, including ethical, moral and economic views.

Present all your findings in your report and give your opinion on whether animals should be kept in zoos.

Use the ACE Learning Ladder to help you do your best.

Use your own words throughout the project.

Use the Good Project Guide sheet for tips on internet safety, research and literacy.

BIOLOGY HOMEWORK TASKS: TASK SHEET (ADVANCED)

ACE LEARNING LADDER

Assessment Check	The types of things you can do:
Advanced	• Write a detailed report, drawing on detailed scientific knowledge and understanding. • Explain scientifically why there is a need to keep animals in zoos, using evidence on endangered animals to justify the points. • Identify a range of ethical or moral issues associated with keeping animals in zoos, offered from people with different viewpoints. • Use evidence to show how a specific zoo breeding programme has impacted on a given animal of your choice. • Explain how zoos have influenced population numbers of endangered animals, and issues that affect their effectiveness. • Use a range of scientific words, symbols and units accurately.
Confident	• Write a report, drawing on scientific knowledge and understanding. • Explain scientifically why there is a need to keep animals in zoos. • Identify ethical or moral issues associated with keeping animals in zoos. • Explain how keeping animals in zoos has provided scientists with evidence to investigate issues or further scientific research. • Explain how zoos influence population numbers of endangered animals. • Use a range of appropriate scientific words, symbols and units.
Establishing	• Write a simple report, drawing on some scientific knowledge and understanding. • State two reasons for keeping animals in zoos. • Give one statement from a person/group who thinks that animals should be kept in zoos and one statement from a person/group who thinks animals should not be kept in zoos. • Describe one animal that has been helped by being kept or bred in a zoo. • Describe how zoos can influence the population of an animal. • Use some appropriate scientific words, symbols and units.

NATIONAL CURRICULUM LINKS

RELATIONSHIPS IN AN ECOSYSTEM
- the interdependence of organisms in an ecosystem, including food webs and insect-pollinated crops
- how organisms affect, and are affected by, their environment, including the accumulation of toxic materials.

WORKING SCIENTIFICALLY
Analysis and evaluation

CROSS–CURRICULAR OPPORTUNITIES INCLUDE:
- citizenship – ethical issues.

TIME

Two homework sessions of between 30 and 60 minutes each, depending on ability.

ASSESSMENT, FEEDBACK AND IMPROVEMENT

Assessing these tasks should not be arduous. Rather than assigning an absolute grade, you should focus on how each student can improve. To ensure that this task is formative, students should be given the opportunity to improve their work based on the teacher's targets or through peer and self-assessment.

GUIDANCE FOR CONFIDENT (C)

Students working with confidence should be able to use evidence about fishing quotas and methods to decide on their suitability.

We find that reading through the project using these additional prompts helps to assess the task.

How does the fish you eat get to your plate? Do you go out and catch it yourself? Probably not! Fishermen work very hard to catch fish to sell on to shops and restaurants, but sometimes they are only allowed to catch a certain amount of fish to sell. If they catch more than this, they often have to throw dead fish back into the sea. Do you think this is a sensible way of fishing? How does it affect marine environments? And are there any fishing methods which are more sustainable?

Write a report on whether fishing quotas are allowing fish to be sustainable. You should:

- Research ways fishermen work to catch fish.
- Find out where fishermen have to follow quotas that say how much they can catch.
- Find out what sustainable fishing is and some examples of where this happens.
- Use the information you find to decide if fishing quotas and methods have any effects on marine environments.
- Decide what your opinion is on whether fishermen should have to stick to quotas, using the information you find to justify your decision.

Use the ACE Learning Ladder to help you do your best.

Use your own words throughout the project.

Use the Good Project Guide sheet for tips on internet safety, research and literacy.

How does the fish you eat get to your plate? Do you go out and catch it yourself? Probably not! Fishermen work very hard to catch fish to sell on to shops and restaurants, but sometimes they are only allowed to catch a certain amount of fish to sell. If they catch more than this, they often have to throw dead fish back into the sea. Do you think this is a sensible way of fishing? How does it affect marine environments? And are there any fishing methods which are more sustainable?

Write a report on whether fishing quotas are allowing fish to be sustainable. You should:
- Research ways fishermen work to catch fish.
- Find out about what fishing quotas are and where they are used.
- Find out if there are sustainable methods of fishing.
- Use the information you find to decide if fishing quotas and methods have any effects on marine environments.
- Decide what your opinion is on fishing quotas and methods, using the information you find to justify your decision.

Use the ACE Learning Ladder to help you do your best.

Use your own words throughout the project.

Use the Good Project Guide sheet for tips on internet safety, research and literacy.

How does the fish you eat get to your plate? Do you go out and catch it yourself? Probably not! Fishermen work very hard to catch fish to sell on to shops and restaurants, but sometimes they are only allowed to catch a certain amount of fish to sell. If they catch more than this, they often have to throw dead fish back into the sea. Do you think this is a sensible way of fishing? How does it affect marine environments? And are there any fishing methods which are more sustainable?

Write a report on whether fishing quotas are allowing fish to be sustainable.

You should prepare a report on fishing methods and fishing quotas, any impacts this has on the marine environment and your view on the issue.

Use the ACE Learning Ladder to help you do your best.

Use your own words throughout the project.

Use the Good Project Guide sheet for tips on internet safety, research and literacy.

BIOLOGY HOMEWORK TASKS: TASK SHEET (ADVANCED)

4

CRITICAL THINKING 6: ACE LEARNING LADDER
FISHING FOLLIES

ACE LEARNING LADDER

Assessment Check	The types of things you can do:
Advanced	• Write a detailed report, drawing on detailed scientific knowledge and understanding. • Explain what a fishing quota is and why quotas are used, providing evidence about their impacts. • Compare fishing techniques that are sustainable and non-sustainable, giving an overall opinion on which you think is best and justifying your decision with evidence. • Explain the consequences of fishing (sustainable and non-sustainable) on the wider environment and society. • Explain how monitoring the effects of fishing may assist marine scientists in their work and state any unintended consequences of fishing quotas. • Use a range of scientific words, symbols and units accurately.
Confident	• Write a report, drawing on scientific knowledge and understanding. • Explain what a fishing quota is and why quotas are used. • Compare fishing techniques that are sustainable and non-sustainable. • Explain the effects fishing and fishing quotas have on different groups and wildlife, including fishermen and fish stocks. • Explain how monitoring the effects of fishing may assist marine scientists in their work. • Use a range of appropriate scientific words, symbols and units.
Establishing	• Write a simple report, drawing on some scientific knowledge and understanding. • State what a fishing quota is. • Give a simple description of what sustainable fishing is. • List the reasons fishing quotas are used. • Give one good and one bad point about the use of fishing quotas. • Use some appropriate scientific words, symbols and units.

NATIONAL CURRICULUM LINKS

Any area may be covered, depending on the area researched.

WORKING SCIENTIFICALLY
Scientific attitudes
Analysis and evaluation

CROSS–CURRICULAR OPPORTUNITIES INCLUDE:
* history – use of sources; considering past developments.

TIME

Two homework sessions of between 30 and 60 minutes each, depending on ability.

ADDITIONAL GUIDANCE

This can be used as a stand-alone task. This is an extremely open-ended task which will offer students scope to research many aspects of science. Students should be encouraged to consider past scientific developments in order to gain perspectives on how the world of science has changed and may change in the future. You may like to spend time in lessons looking through science magazines and journals in order to help students familiarise themselves with current developments. Students will not need to explain ideas in terms of their scientific workings or technologies but should instead focus on the areas of science they feel will be developed over time.

ASSESSMENT, FEEDBACK AND IMPROVEMENT

Assessing these tasks should not be arduous. Rather than assigning an absolute grade, you should focus on how each student can improve. To ensure that this task is formative, students should be given the opportunity to improve their work based on the teacher's targets or through peer and self-assessment.

GUIDANCE FOR CONFIDENT (C)

Students working with confidence can make simple predictions, with justifications.

We find that reading through the project using these additional prompts helps to assess the task.

4 CRITICAL THINKING 7: TASK SHEET (ESTABLISHING)
THE FUTURE OF SCIENCE

Many years ago, we had very different ideas about the world around us. For example, people thought the world was flat and that the Sun orbited the Earth. These ideas may seem silly to us now, but it has only been through scientific research that people's ideas and perceptions have changed. So how will we think differently in the future? Perhaps things we believe now will be proved incorrect.

Write a magazine article about what you think the future holds for science.

You should:
• Investigate how science changes through research, including how it has changed in the past.
• Consider what areas of science you think may see large changes or be the subject of research in the future and why this may be the case.
• Offer ideas about current ideas we have which may change.

Use the ACE Learning Ladder to help you do your best.

Use your own words throughout the project.

Use the Good Project Guide sheet for tips on internet safety, research and literacy.

Many years ago, we had very different ideas about the world around us. For example, people thought the world was flat and that the Sun orbited the Earth. These ideas may seem silly to us now, but it has only been through scientific research that people's ideas and perceptions have changed. So how will we think differently in the future? Perhaps things we believe now will be proved incorrect. Or perhaps the way science itself works will change?

Write a magazine article about what you think the future holds for science.

You should:
- Investigate how science changes through research, including how it has changed in the past.
- Consider what areas of science you think may see large changes or be the subject of research in the future and why this may be the case.
- Offer ideas about current ideas we have which may change.
- Think about how scientists work and whether this may change in the future, giving reasons for your suggestions.

Use the ACE Learning Ladder to help you do your best.

Use your own words throughout the project.

Use the Good Project Guide sheet for tips on internet safety, research and literacy.

BIOLOGY HOMEWORK TASKS: TASK SHEET (CONFIDENT)

THE FUTURE OF SCIENCE

Many years ago, we had very different ideas about the world around us. For example, people thought the world was flat and that the Sun orbited the Earth. These ideas may seem silly to us now, but it has only been through scientific research that people's ideas and perceptions have changed. So how will we think differently in the future? Perhaps things we believe now will be proved incorrect. Or perhaps the way science itself works will change?

Write a magazine article about what you think the future holds for science.

You should:
• Discuss how you think our ideas about science may change over time and how the way scientists work may change, giving reasons for all your suggestions.

Use the ACE Learning Ladder to help you do your best.

Use your own words throughout the project.

Use the Good Project Guide sheet for tips on internet safety, research and literacy.

4

ACE LEARNING LADDER

Assessment Check	The types of things you can do:
Advanced	• Write a detailed magazine article drawing on detailed scientific knowledge and understanding. • Explain the changes you expect to see, using evidence of current research to justify your views. • Explain the major ways in which the world of science has changed in the past and the positive and negative consequences such changes have had and may have in the future. • Explain how the changes you predict would impact on society as a whole, considering both positive and negative consequences. • Give your opinion on whether the predicted changes would be valuable, using evidence to justify your decision. • Use a range of scientific words, symbols and units accurately.
Confident	• Write a magazine article, drawing on scientific knowledge and understanding. • Explain the changes you expect to see, justifying your views. • Explain the major ways in which the world of science has changed in the past and how this influences future changes. • Explain how the changes you predict would impact on society as a whole. • Explain which areas of science would be involved in the changes you predict. • Use a range of appropriate scientific words, symbols and units.
Establishing	• Write a basic magazine article, drawing on some scientific knowledge and understanding. • State what scientific changes you expect to see in the future. • State why you expect to see these changes. • Describe who these changes would affect and why. • Identify the types of scientists that would be involved in your predicted changes. • Use some appropriate scientific words, symbols and units.

CRITICAL THINKING 8: TEACHER NOTES
SCIENTIFIC SPENDING

NATIONAL CURRICULUM LINKS

Any area may be covered, depending on the scientists the student focuses on.

WORKING SCIENTIFICALLY
Scientific attitudes
Analysis and evaluation

CROSS–CURRICULAR OPPORTUNITIES INCLUDE:
 • citizenship – ethical issues.

TIME

Two homework sessions of between 30 and 60 minutes each, depending on ability.

ADDITIONAL GUIDANCE

Students will need access to some information on how science is funded, along with how much is spent annually by the government each year on scientific services. For lower ability students you may wish to provide this information; however, higher ability students should be encouraged to find this data themselves. This will allow them to consider what comes under the umbrella of science; for example, they may wish to include organisations such as the Forensic Science Service along with government research scientists.

ASSESSMENT, FEEDBACK AND IMPROVEMENT

Assessing these tasks should not be arduous. Rather than assigning an absolute grade, you should focus on how each student can improve. To ensure that this task is formative, students should be given the opportunity to improve their work based on the teacher's targets or through peer and self-assessment.

GUIDANCE FOR CONFIDENT (C)

Students working with confidence can present two perspectives and justify their own viewpoint.

We find that reading through the project using these additional prompts helps to assess the task.

Many scientists work for the government. All the scientists have to be paid and they need money in order to carry out research. But what do government scientists do exactly? And how much does the government spend on scientific services each year?

You should:

• Research what government scientists do.
• Find out how much is spent on scientific services each year by the government.
• Give your opinions on the amount spent – do you think it is a fair amount, too much, or too little, and why do you think that?

Write a suggested budget for how you think money should be spent on scientific research, for example:

• Medicine
• Environment
• Military
• Transport.

Use the ACE Learning Ladder to help you do your best.

Use your own words throughout the project.

Use the Good Project Guide sheet for tips on internet safety, research and literacy.

Many scientists work for the government. All the scientists have to be paid and they need money in order to carry out research. But what do government scientists do exactly? And how much does the government spend on scientific services each year?

You should:
- Research what government scientists do.
- Find out how much is spent on scientific services each year by the government.
- Give facts about how the spending is divided up between different areas.
- Give your opinions on the amounts spent – do you think it is a fair amount, too much, or too little, and why do you think that?

Write a suggested budget for how you think money should be spent on scientific research, for example:

- Medicine
- Environment
- Military
- Transport.

Use the ACE Learning Ladder to help you do your best.

Use your own words throughout the project.

Use the Good Project Guide sheet for tips on internet safety, research and literacy.

BIOLOGY HOMEWORK TASKS: TASK SHEET (CONFIDENT)

Many scientists work for the government. All the scientists have to be paid and they need money in order to carry out research. But what do government scientists do exactly? And how much does the government spend on scientific services each year?

You should:
• Research how much money is spent by the government on scientific services each year. Give your opinion on the amount spent and how it is distributed.

Write a suggested budget for how you think money should be spent on scientific research, for example:

• Medicine
• Environment
• Military
• Transport.

Use the ACE Learning Ladder to help you do your best.

Use your own words throughout the project.

Use the Good Project Guide sheet for tips on internet safety, research and literacy.

BIOLOGY HOMEWORK TASKS: TASK SHEET (ADVANCED)

ACE LEARNING LADDER

Assessment Check	The types of things you can do:
Advanced	• Write down your opinions and a budget in detail, drawing on detailed scientific knowledge and understanding. • Explain how you would distribute money in your budget, using evidence to justify why different areas require more or less money. • Evaluate the effectiveness of spending money on scientific research. • Explain how the viewpoints of different groups of people can influence how much money is spent on science. • Explain the benefits, disadvantages and unintended consequences of spending money on scientific research. • Use a range of scientific words, symbols and units accurately.
Confident	• Write down your opinions and a budget, drawing on scientific knowledge and understanding. • Explain how you would distribute money in your budget and how you reached your final figures. • Explain how spending on science could affect different groups of people and society as a whole. • Describe different people's viewpoints on scientific spending. • Explain why spending money on scientific research is essential, giving examples. • Use a range of appropriate scientific words, symbols and units.
Establishing	• Write down your opinions and a simple budget, drawing on some scientific knowledge and understanding. • Show how you would distribute money. • Give reasons for the way you have shared out your budget. • State why spending money on scientific research is important. • Give one advantage and one disadvantage of spending money on scientific research. • Use some appropriate scientific words, symbols and units.

NATIONAL CURRICULUM LINKS

Suitable for any topic area.

WORKING SCIENTIFICALLY
Scientific attitudes
Experimental skills and investigations
Analysis and evaluation

CROSS–CURRICULAR OPPORTUNITIES INCLUDE:
- English – writing a summary, media
- ICT – internet searching, word processing.

TIME

Two homework sessions of between 30 and 60 minutes each, depending on ability.

ADDITIONAL GUIDANCE

This task can be used at any opportunity where there is a science story in the news that students can engage with. You may wish to check that the story matches the generic criteria of the task first.

ASSESSMENT, FEEDBACK AND IMPROVEMENT

Assessing these tasks should not be arduous. Rather than assigning an absolute grade, you should focus on how each student can improve. To ensure that this task is formative, students should be given the opportunity to improve their work based on the teacher's targets or through peer and self-assessment.

GUIDANCE FOR CONFIDENT (C)

Students working with confidence should be able to distinguish between statements that are scientific fact, opinion and speculation.

We find that reading through the project using these additional prompts helps to assess the task.

There is always a story about science in daily newspapers.

Your teacher will give you an article from a newspaper (or an article from an online newspaper).

Read through the article and then read through it again looking for sentences that are fact, opinion and/or speculation.

Imagine you are a scientist – read the article and then write a short summary about it.

- Describe, simply, what the article is about.
- Identify some statements that are scientific facts.
- Identify some statements that are opinions.
- Identify some statements that are speculation.
- Which scientists are named, what is their job and where do they work?
- List what else you would like to know about the topic.

Use the ACE Learning Ladder to help you do your best.

Use your own words throughout the project.

Use the Good Project Guide sheet for tips on internet safety, research and literacy.

4 CRITICAL THINKING 9: TASK SHEET (CONFIDENT)
SCIENCE IN NEWSPAPERS

There is always a story about science in daily newspapers.

Your teacher will give you an article from a newspaper (or an article from an online newspaper).

Read through the article and then read through it again looking for sentences that are fact, opinion and/or speculation.

You are to analyse the article as a scientist and write a short summary.
• Describe, simply, what the article is about.
• Identify some statements that are scientific facts.
• Identify some statements that are opinions.
• Identify some statements that are speculation.
• Which scientists are named, what is their job and where do they work?
• List what else you would like to know about the topic.

Use the ACE Learning Ladder to help you do your best.

Use your own words throughout the project.

Use the Good Project Guide sheet for tips on internet safety, research and literacy.

BIOLOGY HOMEWORK TASKS: TASK SHEET (CONFIDENT)

CRITICAL THINKING 9: TASK SHEET (ADVANCED)
SCIENCE IN NEWSPAPERS

4

There is always a story about science in daily newspapers.

Your teacher will give you an article from a newspaper (or an article from an online newspaper).

Read through the article and then read through it again looking for sentences that are fact, opinion and/or speculation.

You are to analyse the article as a scientist and write a short summary.
- Describe, simply, what the article is about.
- Identify which parts are fact, opinion and speculation.
- Have scientists contributed to the article? How can you tell if they are a reliable source?
- List what else you would like to know about the topic.

Use the ACE Learning Ladder to help you do your best.

Use your own words throughout the project.

Use the Good Project Guide sheet for tips on internet safety, research and literacy.

CRITICAL THINKING 9: ACE LEARNING LADDER
SCIENCE IN NEWSPAPERS

ACE LEARNING LADDER

Assessment Check	The types of things you can do:
Advanced	• Write a detailed summary, drawing on detailed scientific knowledge and understanding. • Explain what the whole article is about (using scientific keywords) and how it relates to wider scientific studies or findings. • Classify some statements as scientific fact, opinion and speculation, explaining your reasons. • Analyse a given scientist's suitability for contributing to the article by finding out about their role, qualifications and other work. • Judge whether the article shows bias, explaining your choice. • Use a range of scientific words, symbols and units accurately.
Confident	• Write a summary, drawing on scientific knowledge and understanding. • Explain what the whole article is about, using scientific keywords. • Classify some statements as scientific fact, opinion and speculation. • Describe how a scientist's work makes them a suitable source of information for the article. • Identify whether the article shows a balanced or unbalanced viewpoint, explaining your choice. • Use a range of appropriate scientific words, symbols and units.
Establishing	• Write a basic summary, drawing on some scientific knowledge and understanding. • State what the article is about. • List one scientific fact, one opinion and one example of speculation from the article. • State the name and job of a scientist in the article. • State one more thing you would like the article to have told you about. • Use some appropriate scientific words, symbols and units.

NATIONAL CURRICULUM LINKS

Suitable for any topic area.

WORKING SCIENTIFICALLY
Scientific attitudes
Experimental skills and investigations
Analysis and evaluation

CROSS–CURRICULAR OPPORTUNITIES INCLUDE:
* English – writing a summary; media, writing for a purpose
* ICT – internet searching, word processing.

TIME

Two homework sessions of between 30 and 60 minutes each, depending on ability.

ADDITIONAL GUIDANCE

This task can be used at any opportunity where there is a science documentary that students can engage with. You may wish to check that the programme matches the generic criteria of the task first.

ASSESSMENT, FEEDBACK AND IMPROVEMENT

Assessing these tasks should not be arduous. Rather than assigning an absolute grade, you should focus on how each pupil can improve. To ensure that this task is formative, students should be given the opportunity to improve their work based on the teacher's targets or through peer and self-assessment.

GUIDANCE FOR CONFIDENT (C)

Students working with confidence should be able to distinguish between statements that are scientific fact, opinion and speculation.

We find that reading through the project using these additional prompts helps to assess the task.

There are many programmes about science on television.

Your teacher will tell you to watch a TV programme.

While you watch the programme, make some notes about these points:
- Describe, simply, what the programme is about.
- Identify some statements that are scientific facts.
- Identify some statements that are opinions.
- Identify some statements that are speculation.
- Are any scientists named? If so, what is their job and where do they work?
- List what else you would like to know about the topic.

Write a review of the TV programme for a science magazine.

Set your review out in the following sections:
- What it was about.
- Who was in it.
- What the main points were.
- What the best bits were.
- What else could have been included.
- A final summary sentence.

Use the ACE Learning Ladder to help you do your best.

Use your own words throughout the project.

Use the Good Project Guide sheet for tips on internet safety, research and literacy.

There are many programmes about science on television.

Your teacher will tell you to watch a TV programme.

While you watch the programme, make some notes about these points:
- Describe, simply, what the programme is about.
- Identify some statements that are scientific facts.
- Identify some statements that are opinions.
- Identify some statements that are speculation.
- Are any scientists named? If so, what is their job and where do they work?
- List what else you would like to know about the topic.

Write a review of the TV programme for a science magazine.

Think about the following points in your review:
- What was it about?
- Who was in it?
- What were the good and bad points about the show?
- Was the topic covered well enough? What else could have been included?
- What is your overall summary?

Use the ACE Learning Ladder to help you do your best.

Use your own words throughout the project.

Use the Good Project Guide sheet for tips on internet safety, research and literacy.

There are many programmes about science on television.

Your teacher will tell you to watch a TV programme.

While you watch the programme, make some notes about these points:
- Describe, simply, what the programme is about.
- Identify some statements that are scientific facts.
- Identify some statements that are opinions.
- Identify some statements that are speculation.
- Are any scientists named? If so what is their job and where do they work?
- List what else you would like to know about the topic.

Write a review of the TV programme for a science magazine.
- First, decide on the structure of the review.

Use the ACE Learning Ladder to help you do your best.

Use your own words throughout the project.

Use the Good Project Guide sheet for tips on internet safety, research and literacy.

SCIENCE ON TV

ACE LEARNING LADDER

Assessment Check	The types of things you can do:
Advanced	• Write a review in detail, drawing on detailed scientific knowledge and understanding. • Explain what the programme is about, using scientific words, and link it to wider scientific research or findings. • Classify and compare statements that are scientific fact, opinion and speculation. • Judge the scientific validity of the programme, explaining your reasons. • Discuss how the main points from the programme could impact on society as a whole. • Use a range of scientific words, symbols and units accurately.
Confident	• Write a review, drawing on scientific knowledge and understanding. • Describe what the programme is about, using scientific words. • Classify statements as scientific fact, opinion and speculation. • Describe the name, job and workplace of a scientist in the programme. • Suggest an improvement to the programme, giving reasons. • Use a range of appropriate scientific words, symbols and units.
Establishing	• Write a basic review, drawing on some scientific knowledge and understanding. • State what the programme is about. • List one scientific fact, an opinion and an example of speculation. • State the name, job and workplace of a scientist in the programme. • State one more thing you would have liked the programme to have told you about. • Use some appropriate scientific words, symbols and units.

4 CRITICAL THINKING 11: TEACHER NOTES
SHAMPOO STATISTICS

NATIONAL CURRICULUM LINKS

Any area may be covered, depending on the statistics selected.

WORKING SCIENTIFICALLY
Scientific attitudes
Analysis and evaluation

CROSS–CURRICULAR OPPORTUNITIES INCLUDE:
- art/media – use of advertising
- maths – use of simple statistics.

TIME

Two homework sessions of between 30 and 60 minutes each, depending on ability.

ADDITIONAL GUIDANCE

Students will need to have learned what statistics are and how they can be used. Before the task it would be a good idea to have a look at some statistics being used, or perhaps carry out a class survey and then produce some statistics from the results obtained. The idea of the task is to consider points such as sample size and misleading advertising, especially in terms of 'scientific' claims.

ASSESSMENT, FEEDBACK AND IMPROVEMENT

Assessing these tasks should not be arduous. Rather than assigning an absolute grade, you should focus on how each student can improve. To ensure that this task is formative, students should be given the opportunity to improve their work based on the teacher's targets or through peer and self-assessment.

GUIDANCE FOR CONFIDENT (C)

Students working with confidence can present two perspectives and justify their own viewpoint.

We find that reading through the project using these additional prompts helps to assess the task.

SHAMPOO STATISTICS

Have you ever noticed products in the shops which make claims like '8 out of 10 cats prefer this food'? Advertisers often use statistics to try and sell you their product by convincing you it is the best available.

Find several examples where statistics have been used (this can be in newspaper articles, adverts, on shampoo bottles, etc.).

Your task is to look at the statistics and decide whether you can trust them and, if so, whether they give you enough information. Write a report on what you find out. You should include examples of the statistics you have looked at. Think about the following points when you prepare your report:

• How many people have been asked? (This is called the sample size.)
• Who has been asked?
• Who worked out the statistics? (Was it the people trying to sell the product?)
• Is there enough information about the statistics?
• What else do you need to know or would you like to know?

Use the ACE Learning Ladder to help you do your best.

Use your own words throughout the project.

Use the Good Project Guide sheet for tips on internet safety, research and literacy.

Have you ever noticed products in the shops which make claims like '8 out of 10 cats prefer this food'? Advertisers often use statistics to try and sell you their product by convincing you it is the best available.

Find several examples where statistics have been used (these can be in newspaper articles, adverts, on shampoo bottles, etc.).

Your task is to examine the statistics and decide whether you can trust them and, if so, whether they are detailed enough. Write a report on what you find out. You should include examples of the statistics you have looked at. Think about the following points when you prepare your report:

- How many people have been asked? (Sample size.)
- Who has been asked?
- Who compiled the statistics? (Was it the people trying to sell the product?)
- Is there enough information about the statistics?
- What else do you need to know?

Use the ACE Learning Ladder to help you do your best.

Use your own words throughout the project.

Use the Good Project Guide sheet for tips on internet safety, research and literacy.

BIOLOGY HOMEWORK TASKS: TASK SHEET (CONFIDENT)

4 SHAMPOO STATISTICS

Have you ever noticed products in the shops which make claims like '8 out of 10 cats prefer this food'? Advertisers often use statistics to try and sell you their product by convincing you it is the best available.

Find several examples where statistics have been used (these can be in newspaper articles, adverts, on shampoo bottles, etc.).

Your task is to examine the statistics and decide whether you can trust them and, if so, whether they are detailed enough. Write a report on what you find out. You should include examples of the statistics you have looked at. Think about the following points when you prepare your report:
- The sample size.
- How the sample was chosen.
- Who the statistics were compiled by.
- The amount of information included with the statistics.
- Any further information required.

Use the ACE Learning Ladder to help you do your best.

Use your own words throughout the project.

Use the Good Project Guide sheet for tips on internet safety, research and literacy.

4 CRITICAL THINKING 11: ACE LEARNING LADDER
SHAMPOO STATISTICS

ACE LEARNING LADDER

Assessment Check	The types of things you can do:
Advanced	• Write a detailed report on examples of statistics, drawing on detailed scientific knowledge and understanding. • Select at least four examples of statistics within adverts, product descriptions or articles. • Explain what the statistics mean, and how this claim may change with differing sample sizes. • Explain how accuracy and reliability are ensured when statistics are compiled and whether your examples demonstrate this. • Identify a range of further information or questions that are needed, explaining why this is the case. • Use a range of scientific words, symbols and units accurately.
Confident	• Write a report on examples of statistics, drawing on scientific knowledge and understanding. • Select at least two examples of statistics within adverts, product descriptions or articles. • Explain what the statistics mean. • Discuss the level of information provided by the statistics and how this affects the reliability and accuracy of any claims made. • Identify further information or questions that are needed, explaining why this is the case. • Use a range of appropriate scientific words, symbols and units.
Establishing	• Write a simple report on examples of statistics, drawing on some scientific knowledge and understanding. • Select one example of statistics within adverts, product descriptions or articles. • State the claim being made by the statistics. • Make one comment on whether the statistics appear reliable or accurate. • Identify one further question you would like to know about the statistics you have chosen. • Use some appropriate scientific words, symbols and units.

Badger Learning
Oldmedow Road
Hardwick Industrial Estate
King's Lynn
PE30 4JJ

Telephone: 01438 791037
Fax: 01438 791036
www.badgerlearning.co.uk

Biology Homework Tasks with Learning Ladders

First published 2014
ISBN 978 1 78464 049 1

**Note: Due to the nature of the internet – it is vital that you check internet links before
they are used in the class room.**

Publisher: Susan Ross
Editor: Danny Pearson
Designer: Adam Wilmott
Cover Design: Big Top Ltd.
Illustrator: Juliet Breese, Aleksandar Sotirovski, Adam Wilmott and Danny Pearson

Printed in the UK
2 4 6 8 10 9 7 5 3 1